CW00544221

between philosophy and music science

Sanja M. Sreckovic

Table of Contents

Chapter 2 – Value of Music_____ 72

Chapter 3 – Emotions in Music_____ 119

Introduction

This dissertation attempts to answer the question: Can experimental results be used as arguments in the philosophical debates? In particular, can the results of experimental psychology and cognitive neuroscience be applied in normative philosophy such as aesthetics?

The greatest motivation in starting this project was to determine the relationship between highly abstract, general and/or normative problems of philosophy on one hand, and the descriptive and highly specific and detailed results of the experimental research on the other hand. I chose aesthetics of music as a case study because it seemed particularly convenient for this kind of enterprise. It is built upon an assortment of abstract and sometimes vague questions such as: What is the meaning of a musical work? What kind of meaning can music possess? How does music communicate its meaning? What makes a musical work valuable? Is aesthetic value inherent to the musical work? Are all aesthetic judgments equally justified? How does music express emotions? How can music evoke emotions in the listeners? The philosophical debates around these issues have lasted for centuries, and it seems, unfortunately, that with time they have not been growing more precise, convincing nor sophisticated.

On the other hand, music is getting increasingly interesting for scientific and experimental research due to its use in medical treatment. Music therapy is used in treating autism, Alzheimer's disease, various forms of dementia, schizophrenia, depression, anxiety disorder, PTSD, aphasia, heart diseases (through stress and anxiety reduction), and also for recovery of motor skills.[1] The empirical literature is getting increasingly enriched with the results of psychological and neurocognitive research on the interactions between music and human cognition and emotions.

---

[1] Stefan Koelsch, "Music-Evoked Emotions: Principles, Brain Correlates, and Implications for Therapy," Annals of the New York Academy of Sciences 1337 (2015): 193-201.

This project is, thus, positioned in the interdisciplinary area between philosophy of music and a number of scientific disciplines that are related to the human body and mind, such as: neuroscience, cognitive science, and experimental psychology. The main subject of the project is the methodological relationship between the philosophical and the empirical examination of music. At the end, the research is supposed to reveal whether the philosophical and the scientific approach to music deal with the same aspects of music, and whether their conclusions can be related to each other. The research presented in this dissertation is supposed to bridge the so-called 'aesthetic-empirical gap' – the gap between the abstract theorizing and the empirical findings concerning music.

History of the Problem

Attempts to empirically approach philosophical questions about music are almost as old as any philosophical thoughts on music. The earliest evidence of the experimental approach to the philosophy of music is found in 4th century BC, in the writings of Aristoxenus, the pupil of Aristotle. Aristoxenus wished to discover what is the essence of music that separates it from non-musical sounds, and what is the quality that makes some music 'melodious', or 'well-tuned', as opposed to the music that lacks this quality. Aristoxenus' (evidently Aristotelian) method consisted, first, in attentive and careful listening to various musical relationships (and this could be only done by a musically practiced researcher with a refined sense of hearing, and then observing and identifying the properties of the melodious music, and finally in applying inductive generalization in order to reach the most general principles which define the essence of music and melodiousness.[2] Aristoxenus proposed an approach to researching music which would focus on the perceptual qualities of musical elements

---

[2] Aristoxenus, "Elementa Harmonica," 1.20, 4.10, and also 32.30-33.39 in *Greek Musical Writings, Volume II: Harmonic and Acoustic Theory*, ed. Andrew Barker (Cambridge University Press, 1989), pp. 126-128, 150-151.

perceived by the listeners, instead of classifying them solely by their formal properties such as magnitudes.[3]

This kind of empirical practice in investigating music was revived in the 19th century, together with the birth of experimental psychology. The 1870s brought a rebirth of ideas about experimentally investigating (both visual and auditive) perception, beauty, and aesthetic appeal, and the ideas of that period inspire most of today's methodology in experimental research of music.[4] The emergence of laboratory psychology in the 19th century involved the creation of methods for the quantitative measurement of mental processes. The first methods, rationale, and systematic use of mental measurement was essentially the contribution of one person – Gustav Fechner.[5] The first volume of Fechner's *Elemente der Psychophysik*, which he called "outer psychophysics," was devoted to investigating functional relationships between the magnitudes of physical stimuli and the sensations, and its aim was reaching general laws of the relationship between the physical stimuli and the sensations, and finally between the physical and the psychological sphere.[6] The second volume, called "inner psychophysics," concerned the nature of the relationship between sensations and the neurological activity in the brain. Fechner was seriously restricted in this research by the inaccessibility of neurological processes and the insufficiently developed state of neuroscience. However, in pursuing his goal, Fechner had "incidentally introduced mental measurement into psychology."[7] The next step in developing the empirical approach to music perception began with Hermann Helmholtz who attempted to find associations between the aesthetic

---

[3] Aristoxenus, *op. cit.*, 48-48.30, pp. 161-162.

[4] Daniel J. Levitin and Anna K. Tirovolas, "Current Advances in the Cognitive Neuroscience of Music" *Annals of the New York Academy of Sciences* 1156 (2009), p. 211. See also Marcus T. Pearce et al., "Neuroaesthetics: The Cognitive Neuroscience of Aesthetic Experience," *Perspectives on Psychological Science* 11, no. 2 (2016), p. 266.

[5] Robert H. Wozniak, "Introduction to Elemente der Psychophysik," in *Classics in Psychology, 1855-1914: Historical Essays*, ed. Robert H. Wozniak (Bristol, UK: Thoemmes Press, 1999).

[6] *Ibid.*

[7] *Ibid.*

qualities of musical elements (such as notes, intervals or scales) with their 'psychoacoustic properties'.[8] By the latter he understood frequencies of the simple tones (or sine waves) which constitute complex tones, and the ratios between their frequencies.[9] Many studies of the early phase of experimental psychology were dedicated to music, and one of the motivating factors behind forming the Gestalt movement in psychology was examining the relationships between the whole and its parts in music and melody.[10]

The last couple of decades have brought an exponential increase in research on the cognitive capacities involved in human interaction with music. These studies focus on 'musical behaviors' such as listening to music, remembering musical sequences, music performance, musical training, composing music, dancing, movement, etc.[11] The increased use of neuroimaging along with neurological case studies brought about the crucial paradigm shift in investigating the neurological basis of musical behaviors.[12] Due to the recent development of science and technology, the functioning of the human brain has come within reach of empirical observations, and this has also affected the possibilities in experimentally researching music.[13] Most of the experimental research on music was primarily motivated by the application of the results for medical therapy of neurological and similar disorders.[14] In addition, there is

[8] Elvira Brattico and Marcus T. Pearce. "The Neuroaesthetics of Music." *Psychology of Aesthetics, Creativity, and the Arts* 7 (2013), p.48.

[9] *Ibid.*

[10] Levitin and Tirovolas, *op. cit.*, p. 211, referring to Christian von Ehrenfels, "On Gestalt qualities," in *Foundations of Gestalt Theory*, ed. Barry Smith (Munich: Philosphia Verlag, 1988. Original work published in 1890).

[11] Levitin and Tirovolas, *ibid.*

[12] Levitin and Tirovolas, *op. cit.*, p. 211. Also see Stefan Koelsch, "Brain Correlates of Music-Evoked Emotions," *Nature Reviews Neuroscience* 15, no. 3 (2014): 170-180.

[13] Anjan Chatterjee, "Neuroaesthetics: A coming of age story," Journal of Cognitive Neuroscience 23 (2011): 53-62.

[14] Koelsch, "Music-Evoked Emotions: Principles, Brain Correlates, and Implications for Therapy." See also Braticco and Pearce, *op. cit.*, p. 57.

increasingly more interest for understanding the functional neuroanatomy of the human processing of music with the help of different technologies such as fMRI, PET, ERP, MEG, and brain lesion studies. Various methods of medical diagnostics and neurological case studies have been used in experimental observation of human relationship with music, specifically, in determining the neurological basis of the activities and reactions concerning music.[15]

Contemporary Attitudes

There is currently no consensus regarding the question if this kind of research, even if it does arrive at some conclusive results, can tell us anything relevant to the philosophy of music. A number of authors have welcomed the experimental psychology and neuroscience of music.[16] Some of them even argue that "aesthetic philosophy is receding to a sideline 'advisory' role, while cognitive science takes an unaccustomed leadership position."[17] Others, however, claim that the neurological approach has nothing to contribute to philosophy of art in general.[18] The attitudes toward this question span from one radical view to the other – with little in-between. One group of thinkers refutes the possibility that natural sciences could give any relevant account of music and art in general. They offer various reasons: science can

---

[15] Koelsch, "Brain Correlates of Music-Evoked Emotions."

[16] Noël Carroll, Margaret Moore, and Willian P. Seeley, "The Philosophy of Art and Aesthetics, Psychology, and Neuroscience: Studies in Literature, Music, and Visual Arts," in *Aesthetic Science: Connecting Minds, Brains, and Experience*, ed. Arthur P. Shimamura and Stephen E. Palmer (New York, NY: Oxford University Press, 2011), pp. 31-62.

[17] Brattico and Pearce, *op. cit.*, p.49., referring to David Huron, "Aesthetics," in *Oxford Handbook of Music Psychology*, ed. Susan Hallam, Ian Cross, and Michael Thaut (New York, NY: Oxford University Press. 2010), p. 151.

[18] See Raymond Tallis, "The Limitations of a Neurological Approach to Art," *The Lancet* 372 (2008): 19-20.

never encompass the specific essence of art, or its creativity or diversity,[19] nor can it touch upon normative questions on art.[20]

Others critique scientific explanations of musical phenomena given hitherto for being overly reductionistic, mechanicistic, or musically or psychologically simplistic (e.g., they attempt to explain music cognition by testing the reactions to isolated single notes). These criticisms point to the fact that the scientific accounts of music are based on understanding musical works solely as a source of stimuli which affect certain areas of the brain, and thus leave out everything we really care to know about music as an art form.[21] Fierce attitudes on the neuroscientific explanations of art are reflected in claims such as that neuroaesthetics is the ultimate expression of faith in neuroscientism,[22] or in the book titles such as "Brainwashed: The Seductive Appeal of Mindless Neuroscience," and "Aping Mankind: Neuromania, Darwinitis and the Misrepresentation of Humanity."

On the other extreme, some authors believe that scientific disciplines such as biology, neuroscience, and psychology are not only able to explain all significant problems and questions on music much more successfully than philosophical or musicological theories, but they can also explain them away, i.e. reveal them as trivial or meaningless.[23] Steven Pinker famously wrote that music cognition is "not worth studying" because music is only "auditory cheesecake," an "evolutionary byproduct

---

[19] Alva Noë, "Art and the Limits of Neuroscience," *New York Times*, Dec. 4, 2011.; Also see Tallis, *op. cit.*

[20] Katherine Tullman and Nada Gatalo, "Cave Paintings, Neuroaesthetics and Everything in Between: An Interview With Noël Carroll," *Postgraduate Journal of Aesthetics* 9, no. 1, 2012.

[21] Ian Cross and Irène Deliège, "Introduction: Cognitive Science and Music – An Overview," *Contemporary Music Review*, 9:1-2, (1993): pp. 1-6.

[22] Tallis, *op. cit.*

[23] Ivor Armstrong Richards, *Poetries and Sciences: A Reissue with a Commentary of Science and Poetry* (1926, 1935) (New York: W. W. Norton and Company, 1970); See also Steven Pinker, *How The Mind Works*, (London: Allen Lane, 1997), p. 534.

of the adaptation for human language."[24] Pinker's claim that the arts are 'pleasure technologies,' i.e. technologies for stimulating brain areas which induce a feeling of pleasure by (artificially) signaling the presence of adaptively valuable objects (such as food, shelter, partner, environment information, etc.), Pinker explained art in general by evolutionary mechanisms. Methodologically, this kind of explanation implies that the development of biology and cognitive science can explain at once the human relationship with the arts, along with any other pleasure-inducing objects in the environment. This version of a reductionist approach renders all other attempts to establish value or meaning in art unnecessary or pointless.[25]

These discrepancies can be attributed to a lack of communication between music theorists and philosophers of music on one side, and experimental psychologists and neuroscientists on the other side. Recently, however, the circumstances have changed. John Sloboda has pronounced in 1986 that "the psychology of music has come of age,"[26] after the publication of 'Generative Theory of Tonal Music' in 1983, Lerdahl's and Jackendoff's seminal work which offers an empirically informed, highly sophisticated musicological theory.[27] This 'coming of age' can even more rightly be claimed today, after 33 years of technological and scientific development.

---

[24] Levitin and Tirovolas, *op. cit.*, p. 212. See also Pinker, *op. cit.* 528-538.

[25] Pinker, *op. cit.* 528-538.

[26] John A. Sloboda, "Cognition and Real Music: The Psychology of Music Comes of Age," *Psychologica Belgica* 26 (1986): 199-219.

[27] Cross and Deliège, *op. cit.*, p. 2.

My Contribution

I believe that the radical attitudes are premature. The implications of scientific findings have not yet been thoroughly examined and systematized in order to be properly connected to the philosophical issues. In a terrain characterized by strong mutually opposing attitudes where no firm ground has yet been established, my research aims to clarify the relationships between the scientific and the philosophical claims about music. I present a way to bridge the aesthetic-empirical gap and explore the potential contribution of empirical research to the aesthetic debates. The aim of my dissertation is not to use the empirical results to "solve" the philosophical debates, or to defend any of the offered philosophical theories. Instead, my research should contribute to understanding whether the experimental results can be relevant to understanding certain aspects of art, and if so, to which degree. In addition, I show the unexpected contribution of the experimental research in that it enriches the philosophical theories of music with new possibilities, and imposes demands on conceptual precision in formulating the debated issues. The contribution of the dissertation is thus methodological, in the sense that it reveals the relationships and the mutual influences between the methods of different, and seemingly very distant disciplines.

Methodological Idea: 'Operationalization'

The gap between the two disciplines widely considered as remote and perhaps incompatible is not easy to bridge. One obvious obstacle in attempting to connect the aesthetic views with potentially relevant empirical results is the inevitable transition from the normative to the descriptive claims. On one side of the gap, the results and conclusions of the neurocognitive studies rely on descriptive, empirical claims, and measurable phenomena. On the other side, the questions of philosophical aesthetics of music are either normative in nature, or highly abstract and remote from being measurable.

I propose a way to bridge the aesthetic-empirical gap through an analysis of the normative aesthetic concepts which reveals their descriptive, empirically measurable counterparts. This requires tracing the relationships between the mutually related concepts of the aesthetic and the empirical level. My method consists in implementing an *operationalization* of the normative and other specifically aesthetical concepts in a way that renders them approachable through the empirically measurable phenomena. I attempt this by adopting the dispositionalist approach toward the aesthetic concepts. I propose that the aesthetic concepts should be understood dispositionally, in the sense that they refer to both the objective properties of musical works and the appropriate reactions of the perceiving subjects.

The aesthetic theories involve concepts such as beauty, value, form and content, which are almost exclusively applied to the objects, i.e. musical works. These theories discuss, for example, aesthetic value of a musical work, or the relationship between form and content in music. When understood dispositionally, these concepts are brought into a relationship with the perceiving subjects. Thus the aesthetic value of a musical work makes the work suitable to be preferred and recognized as valuable by the listeners, and the meaning of a certain aspect of the work makes the work suitable to be recognized as meaningful by the perceiving subjects. Implementing operationalization through the dispositionalist approach establishes conceptual relationships between the aesthetic concepts on one side, and the terms used in the experimental research, and applied the subjects, i.e. listeners, such as pleasure, preference, and also the perception of syntax and semantics. By establishing relationships between the objective and subjective counterparts of the aesthetic concepts, I reveal the empirical indicators of the theoretically evasive phenomena referred to by the aesthetic concepts. Thus, the aesthetic concepts such as value, meaning, form and content are approachable through the related descriptive inter-subjective concepts, and the aesthetic-empirical gap can be successfully bridged.

More specifically, I propose to approach the concept of value through the (empirically measurable) preference shown by the proficient listener (the Humean "good critic"). The concept of beauty is approached through the "particular kind of pleasure" (measured by the self-reports and the physiological reactions of the listeners). The aesthetical concepts of form and content, typically applied to artworks, can be approached through the perception of syntax and semantics of the recipients, which can also be measured by physiological markers of syntactic and semantic processing known from other fields of research. The method will be presented in more detail and shown at work in each chapter of the dissertation.

For each particular philosophical problem discussed in the dissertation, I demonstrate that the experimental results indeed provide interesting insights which can be fruitfully analyzed for further philosophical treatment of the given problems. I conclude that philosophers can benefit from examining experimental studies, not only regarding the particular aesthetic theories, but also in regard to the methodological consideration, since it is repeatedly shown in the dissertation that the interdisciplinary approach I present uncovers methods which can be immensely useful to philosophers, but are not commonly available from the armchair philosophical approach.

Overview of the Chapters

The dissertation consists of three chapters. Each chapter deals with one particular problem in philosophy of music: meaning in music, value of music, and the relationship between music and the emotions. The common core of all three chapters is establishing connections between philosophical discussions of music and the results provided by studies in experimental psychology, neuroscience and cognitive science.

Each chapter begins with a brief presentation of the philosophical debates and the main theories concerning the respective problem. The philosophical part is followed by more detailed presentations of the experimental studies which provide results relevant for the philosophical theories. Finally, each chapter ends with a commentary of the ways in which the experimental results contribute to the philosophical debates. I discuss the implications for the philosophical theories, but also emphasize the methodological insights gained from combining the philosophical and the experimental approach.

In the first chapter I focus on the issue of meaning in music. The questions which define this problem are: How do we determine the meaning of a musical work? What kind of meaning arises from music? Does music have syntax and semantics? Can music represent extra-musical phenomena and events? Can music convey conceptual content? In this chapter I show how by measuring neurological reactions, and physiological measures (e.g., skin conductance level, respiratory rate, heart rate, etc.) the experimental studies provide interesting suggestions concerning the existence of *musical* syntax and semantics, and that musical structure alone can through its features influence the general emotional arousal of the listeners.

The second chapter deals with aesthetic value of music, through questions such as: Where lies the value of a musical work? Does aesthetic value inhere in the musical work or is it only assigned to it by the subjects? Do aesthetic judgments possess truth value and truth conditions? I briefly present the objectivist and the subjectivist approach to these questions, and proceed to the dispositionalist view which allows for more interesting possibilities in philosophical treatment of the issue of value, and also enables the philosophical claims to be connected to the empirical research. I argue that the numerous studies on musical expertise and various cognitive capacities show that there are significant differences among the music listeners, which supports the claim of the dispositionalists that there may be epistemically privileged subjects in judging the value of musical works. Unfortunately, the preferences of the subjects in the experimental body of work are not understood in the way that fits the sense of preference which would be relevant for the aesthetic value, but I propose a way in which the next step can be taken in order to reach the conclusions which would be relevant.

The third chapter concerns musical emotions. The philosophers mostly deal with the relationship between music and the emotions by trying to define musical expressiveness. Another, less popular debate concerns the question of the capability of music to induce genuine ('everyday') emotions in the listeners. This chapter, unfortunately, does not provide us with insights as interesting as the insights of the other two chapters. I show that the concept of musical expressiveness is not successfully defined and does not seem to be suitable for being included in the empirical research. The issue of expressiveness has, however, been paid so much attention by the philosophers of music, leading to vigorous debates, that I felt it needed to be a part of the dissertation, at least in order to show that the attempts of the philosophers to find a precise definition of musical expressiveness are unsuccessful, if not futile. As opposed to that, I also show that the debate on musical induction of emotions can be resolved by the empirical studies, only to have the results of the studies confirm the intuition of the majority of philosophers of music – that music does, indeed, induce emotions.

Additional Notes

It will be noticed that the experiments are presented in greater detail than is usual in even the most empirically oriented philosophical works. The reason behind these extensive presentations is to highlight the importance of methodological specificities of the experimental studies, which enable reaching conclusions concerning the philosophical problems unavailable from the philosophical approach alone. An additional reason is to enable the readers (assumed to be mostly unacquainted with the technical aspects of experimental psychology) to understand, step by step, how the experimental methods enable us to reach such conclusions. My intention in all three chapters is to provide a comprehensive presentation of the procedures of the experiments, and go further than solely citing their conclusions. Readers with a philosophical background but unacquainted with the experimental methodology should be able to see for themselves not only that the methodology behind the experimental conclusions is sound, but also to follow the steps toward the relevant conclusions, and observe the types of arguments provided by the experimental studies.

Chapter 1 – Meaning in Music

The appraisal of a piece of music involves two main components: first, understanding the content (meaning) of the musical work, and, second, judging its value – perhaps not necessarily in that order. This chapter will focus on the first component, and examine the contribution of empirical research to the philosophical debates on musical meaning. This chapter will open by presenting the key claims of the most notable philosophical accounts on musical meaning: *formalism*, *expressionism*,[28] and a more complex and less polemical account offered by Leonard B. Meyer, which I will call *pluralism*.

Recent studies of behavioral and neurological reactions to musical stimuli have revealed the complex relationships between the processing of syntax, semantics and emotion in music, and these results may have interesting implications for the question about the kind of meaning present in music. This chapter will focus on three such studies. The first study provides evidence that the features of musical structure itself affect semantic processing in the listeners, thereby implying the possibility of specifically musical meaning, crucial for the formalist view.[29] The second study establishes connections between particular features of musical structure and the emotions evoked by music, supporting Meyer's claim that music itself might convey emotional meaning, without the help of the extra-musical indicators such as titles, text, etc., and even of customary associations between musical elements (such as

---

[28] 'Expressionism' in this context does not refer to the art movement, but instead refers to the view on the meaning in music, as defined by Meyer – see Leonard B. Meyer, *Emotion and meaning in music* (Chicago: University of Chicago Press, 1956), pp. 2-3.

[29] Nikolaus Steinbeis and Stefan Koelsch, "Shared Neural Resources between Music and Language Indicate Semantic Processing of Musical Tension-Resolution Patterns," *Cerebral Cortex* 18, no. 5 (2008): 1169-78.

major or minor chord) and particular emotions.[30] The third and perhaps the most interesting study demonstrates a relationship between the features of musical structure and conceptual content usually attributed to language, implying the possibility that musical structure alone might even convey conceptual meaning, denied by most philosophers of music, regardless of their personal inclinations in the meaning debates.[31] I conclude that the implications of the experimental research reveal that the issue of musical meaning is far more complex than was implicitly supposed in the philosophical debates, and also suggest new ways to enrich the classical philosophical debate on the meaning in music.

---

[30] Nikolaus Steinbeis, Stefan Koelsch, and John Sloboda, "The Role of Harmonic Expectancy Violations in Musical Emotions: Evidence from Subjective, Physiological, and Neural Responses," *Journal of Cognitive Neuroscience*, 18, no. 8 (2006): 1380-93.

[31] Stefan Koelsch et al., "Music, Language and Meaning: Brain Signatures of Semantic Processing," *Nature Neuroscience*, no. 7 (2004): 302-7.

1 Philosophical Theories of Meaning in Music

Musicological discussions have focused mostly on the question whether music is capable of communicating meaning, and if it is, whether meaning arises because of the associations between musical elements and the extra-musical world, or because music has its own, unique, set of symbols.[32] Instead of asking "how" (by which means) music communicates, philosophers, however, were always more interested in asking "what" music communicates – what kind of meaning arises from music: whether it is specifically musical, emotional, or some other type of meaning. The answers to the latter question can be very roughly summarized into three broad views, where the first two postulate one specific type of meaning: emotional and specifically musical, while the third, pluralistic view offers a more sophisticated and complex account of the aspects of meaning in music.

1.1 Expressionism

Many philosophers define the value of music by appealing to human emotions, and likewise define the understanding of music through the emotions it expresses, or evokes in its listeners. It has been noticed since Antiquity that music can evoke various feelings, ranging from joy, happiness, serenity, calmness, to apathy, melancholy, sadness or sorrow, and that, in turn, emotions have a strong influence on human beings and their morality and character. Already Plato establishes associations of musical modes and the moral characteristics. Plato describes the Lydian mode as the 'wailing mode', and allows in his ideal republic only "two modes – a violent one and a voluntary one, which will produce the finest imitation of the sounds of (...) moderate and courageous men."[33] Aristotle similarly writes that "even in mere melodies there is an imitation of character, for the musical modes differ essentially from one another, and those who hear them are differently affected by each. Some of them make men sad and grave, like the so-called Mixolydian, others enfeeble the

---

[32] Steinbeis and Koelsch, "Shared Neural Resources," 1169.

[33] See Plato, *Republic*, 398d-99b.

mind (...), another, again, produces a moderate and settled temper, which appears to be peculiar effect of the Dorian; the Phrygian inspires enthusiasm."[34] He concludes the passage with the words: "Enough has been said to show that music has a power of forming the character, and should therefore be introduced into the education of the young."[35] Regarding music mostly from the ethical or rather pedagogical point of view extended well into to the 18th and 19th centuries.[36] In this long-lasting tradition, it is believed that the value of music resides in its emotional, and thus moral effect upon the listeners, and music that lacks appropriate emotional effects is considered almost worthless, regardless of its perceived beauty or the pleasure it elicits.[37] The ancient conviction that specific musical elements, such as scales, intervals, types of metrics, etc., correspond to specific emotions and moods, is echoed in the more recent writings as well.[38] The composers of the Enlightenment period were extensively instructed to utilize their knowledge of these correspondences, and of the emotional effects of musical elements in order to evoke the (morally) appropriate emotions in their listeners.[39]

---

[34] Aristotle, *Politics*, VIII 5, 1340a.

[35] Aristotle, *op. cit.*, 1340b.

[36] See Johann Georg Sulzer, "General Theory of the Fine Arts (1771-74): Selected Articles," in *Aesthetics and the Art of Musical Composition in the German Enlightenment: Selected Writings of Johann Georg Sulzer and Heinrich Christoph Koch*, ed. Nancy Baker, Thomas Christensen (Cambridge University Press, 2006), pp. 25-111.

[37] Wladyslaw Tatarkiewicz, *A History of Six Ideas: An Essay in Aesthetics* (Polish Scientific Publishers-Warszawa, 1980), pp. 23-5.

[38] Sulzer, "General Theory of the Fine Arts," p. 81., and also Heinrich Christoph Koch, "Introductory Essay on Composition (1787)," in *Aesthetics and the Art of Musical Composition in the German Enlightenment: Selected Writings of Johann Georg Sulzer and Heinrich Christoph Koch*, ed. Nancy Baker, Thomas Christensen (Cambridge University Press, 2006), pp. 144-188.

[39] See Sulzer, "General Theory of the Fine Arts," p. 50-4., and also Johann Mattheson, *Johann Mattheson's Der vollkommene Capellmeister: a revised translation with critical commentary*, ed. by Ernest C. Harriss and Ann Arbor (Mich: UMI Research Press, c1981), p. 104, §54.

This context of thinking about music is probably what led many authors to think of the meaning in music primarily in emotional terms. We cannot truly regard these views as theories of meaning in music. They should more rightly be regarded as a more or less confused compound of beliefs regarding the emotional effect and, accordingly, moral and educational purpose of music, connected to the assumed correspondences between musical elements and particular emotions. Thus, aside from attempting to establish these kinds of correspondences, the older expressionist theories do not offer a detailed analysis of the meaning aspect of music.

One different expressionist approach to musical value and meaning treats music as the vehicle of expression of sincere subjective emotions, regardless of the moral effect. This principally Romanticist view is echoed in many contemporary works on the aesthetics of music, and is formulated in its most distinctive form as the view that many musical works should be interpreted as psychological dramas – as an expression of the emotional processes attributed either to the composer, or to the "persona" – the implied author of the musical work, not necessarily coinciding with the composer.[40]

I will accordingly illustrate the expressionist view by presenting fundamental claims of some recent, conceptually far more sophisticated theories. Namely, in her account of musical expressiveness, Jenefer Robinson claims that some musical works possess an expressive structure which can and should be understood as a development of psychological events in time, and in order for this sequence of events to form an organic whole, she postulates the persona, a quasi-person to whom we attribute all these psychological events.[41] This is in fact a version of the Expression theory (see Chapter 3) which evades the empirical problems of the Expression theory by dispensing with the actual composer's emotions. Instead of attributing the emotions

---

[40] See Jenefer Robinson, *Deeper than Reason: Emotion and its Role in Literature, Music and Art* (Oxford: Clarendon Press, 2005), and also Jerrold Levinson, "Hope in The Hebrides", Music, Art, and Metaphysics (Ithaca, NY: Cornell University Press, 1990), 336-75.

[41] See Robinson, *Deeper than Reason*, p. 307. and also Gregory Karl and Jenefer Robinson, "Shostakovich's Tenth Symphony and the Musical Expression of Cognitively Complex Emotions", *Journal of Aesthetics and Art Criticism*, 53 (1995), 401-415.

heard in the music to the composer, they are instead attributed to the persona whom we imagine expressing those emotions. Music can convey all of that emotional content "through complex movements of harmony, melody, and rhythm."[42]

Robinson claims that music is able to mirror the key aspects of an emotional process through mirroring vocal expressions and motor activity characteristic of particular emotions. She attempts to support this claim by analyzing musical examples and, similarly to her predecessors, by detecting correspondences between musical elements and aspects of emotions, e.g. major modes, consonances, and tonal movements upward are associated with positive emotions, while minor modes, dissonances, and downward movements are associated with negative emotions. Likewise, similarity or contrast of the musical material between certain sections of a musical piece can be interpreted as similarity or contrast of emotional states expressed by those sections.[43] Interpreting musical meaning in emotional terms is, according to Robinson, only one possible way of interpreting certain musical works. There can be several mutually incompatible interpretations, where each interpretation would reveal different aspects of music.[44] Jerrold Levinson goes even further, and claims that music can express "higher" or cognitively complex emotions.[45] Even though he agrees with the proponents of the opposing view such as Hanslick that music cannot convey the conceptual content of emotions (or conceptual content in general),[46] Levinson believes that, by conveying enough of the other aspects of a certain emotion, music can lead an experienced listener to regularly think of that emotion as a response to the relevant musical piece.[47]

---

[42] Robinson in fact applies to music the notion of the implied author originally suggested in literary theory. See Robinson, *Deeper than Reason*, Part Two: Emotion in Literature, pp. 105-228.

[43] Robinson, *Deeper than Reason*, pp. 311-12.

[44] Robinson, *Deeper than Reason*, pp. 333-6.

[45] Levinson, "Hope in the Hebrides," p. 336.

[46] Eduard Hanslick, *On the Musically Beautiful*, trans. Geoffrey Payzant (Indianapolis: Hackett Publishing Company, 1986.), p. 10.

[47] Levinson, "Hope in the Hebrides," pp. 344-57.

In short, this group of theories, although with different specifics and motivations, define musical meaning in terms of the emotions the music represents, expresses, or evokes in its listeners. The question "what music means" is answered by naming the emotions associated in any of those ways with the musical work in question.

1.2 Formalism

Another group of theories opposes this belief with the claim that the value of music is independent of (and even unrelated to) the emotions, either felt or perceived in music,[48] and define musical value only by appealing to the structural aspects of music, such as its artistic beauty.[49] The formalists tie both value and meaning of music to the musical structure itself, and disregard the emotional effects that might arise out of it. In addition, it is claimed that music is not even able to represent emotions. According to the formalists, the criterion which distinguishes an emotion from other emotions is its conceptual content, constituted by a number of conceptions and judgments associated with the concept of that emotion.[50] Therefore, e.g., "the feeling of hope cannot be separated from the representation of a future happy state which we compare with the present," or "love cannot be thought without the representation of a beloved person, without desire and striving after felicity," etc.[51] Without such conceptual components, the representations of emotions are reduced to the intensity and the dynamics. The latter are, however, not unique for an emotion. Different emotions may have the same intensity and dynamics. In addition, one and the same emotion may vary in intensity and dynamics.[52] Emotions, therefore, cannot be specified without representing conceptual content. Finally, since pure instrumental music cannot

---

[48] Hanslick, *op. cit.*, pp. 3-7

[49] Hanslick, *op. cit.*, pp. 31-5.

[50] Hanslick, *op. cit.*, p. 9. Also see Sanja Srećković, „Eduard Hanslick's Formalism and His Most Influential Contemporary Critics," *Belgrade Philosophical Annual* 27 (2014), p. 117-18.

[51] Hanslick, *op. cit.*, p. 9.

[52] *Ibid.*, p. 9. Also see Srećković, „Eduard Hanslick's Formalism," p. 117.

reproduce concepts, as they are "not within the scope of music,"[53] the formalists conclude that music is not able to represent emotions.[54]

Thus, instead of focusing on the emotional effects, the formalists focus on the *form*, which in music consists only in tonal structures and tonal relationships. Formalistic view is based on the more general idea that the value of each art cannot be separated from the characteristics of its particular form and technique (e.g. tones in music, words in literature, color in painting, etc.). In application to music, what makes a composition good or bad is whether it is constructed out of beautiful tone-forms or not.[55] Thus, the value of music is defined solely by appealing to tonal relationships, irrespective of some extra-musical content, references, or effects. The formalistic view on musical value is bound together with the belief that musical meaning should also be sought in musical form. Formalists believe that any proper understanding of musical meaning must focus on the tonal structure. According to Eduard Hanslick, the most eloquent proponent of formalism, music "is a kind of language which we speak and understand yet cannot translate."[56] It is important, however, to note that it is a language which expresses musical, and not extra-musical thoughts. The analogy between music and language is limited by the crucial difference between them, which lies in the fact that "in speech the sound is only a sign, that is, a means to an end which is entirely distinct from that means, while in music the sound is an object, i.e., it appears to us as an end in itself."[57] Hanslick insists that music does possess sense and logic, but these are uniquely *musical* sense and logic. The trained listener, well acquainted with musical logic would thus quickly distinguish between genuine musical thoughts and 'empty phrases'.[58]

---

[53] Hanslick, *op. cit.*, p. 9.

[54] Hanslick, *op. cit.*, p. 9-10

[55] Hanslick, *op. cit.*, p. 35.

[56] Hanslick, *op. cit.*, 30.

[57] Hanslick, *op. cit.*, 42.

[58] Hanslick, *op. cit.*, 30.

Hanslick articulates the formalistic view most successfully in explaining that the idea created in the artist's imagination, to be expressed in his work, "is a tonal idea, not a conceptual [or any other extra-musical] idea which has (...) been translated into tones."[59] He adds that musical ideas are "an end in itself", not a vehicle to represent extra-musical ideas related to emotions or concepts.[60] According to the various examples from the history of music, it seems that, for Hanslick, these ideas consist in constructing tonal structures, skillfully manipulating the relationships between tones, chords, smaller and larger structures, generating musical expectations of the listener, often referring to other musical ideas – through repetitions, variations, extensions, contrast, elaboration, and other musical techniques.[61]

The crucial idea of formalism is that the content of music *is* the form of music: "Music consists of tonal sequences, tonal forms; these have no other content than themselves."[62] The relationship between content and form does not consist in a translation of the former (some extra-musical content) to the latter (tonal forms), or a representation of one by another. Rather, it consists in elaboration: an unrefined tonal idea (the content of the composition) is elaborated and refined until it reaches its final form.[63] The content, i.e. the meaning of music is thus inseparable from musical form. In another illustrative formulation, "music speaks not merely by means of tones, it speaks only tones."[64] In short, musical structure is both what expresses the meaning in music, and what the music means. The meaning in music is exhausted by the musical ideas.

---

[59] Hanslick, *op. cit.*, p. 32

[60] Hanslick, *op. cit.*, 28.

[61] Hanslick, *op. cit.*, 33.

[62] Hanslick, *op. cit.*, 78.

[63] Hanslick, *op. cit.*, 35

[64] Hanslick, *op. cit.*, 78.

1.3 Meyer's Pluralism

As already mentioned, Meyer proposes a pluralistic account of meaning which is intended more as a clarification of the various possibilities of meaning in music than as an advocacy of the primacy or existence of just one kind of meaning. Meyer explains the controversy between the formalists and the expressionists as a result of a tendency of the proponents of both sides toward "philosophical monism," rather than being a result of any logical incompatibility. He attributes the source of the confusion to the tendency (also on both sides) to locate meaning exclusively in one aspect of the communicative process, and firmly states that the same stimulus (such as any musical event) may have many different meanings.[65] With this in view, he makes several important distinctions.

First, he attempts to reconcile two opposing views on the *source* of musical meaning. The 'referentialist' view, which holds that musical meaning is *designative* in that it lies in the relationship between musical 'signs' and extra-musical objects. Musical events, according to the referentialists (such as the expressionists), refer to (or designate) the extra-musical realm, that is, to concepts, emotions, or other extra-musical events.[66]

The 'absolutist' view, on the other hand, states that musical meaning is *non-designative* in that it remains entirely within the context of the musical work – in the musical processes themselves. Meyer accuses the proponents of this view (i.e. the formalists) of the lack of clarity and precision concerning how exactly meaning arises out of non-designative sequence of musical stimuli[67] (and he himself offers a possible explanation by appealing to tension-resolution processes – see below). Nevertheless, Meyer accepts both types of meaning posited by these two views, and calls the first,

---

[65] Meyer, *op. cit.*, 33-4.

[66] Meyer, *op. cit.*, 33.

[67] Meyer, *loc. cit.*

posited by the absolutists, 'intramusical' meaning, and the second, posited by the referentialists, 'extra-musical' meaning.[68]

Meyer observes another important distinction within intramusical meaning, namely, that it can be both 'intellectual' and 'emotional'. The distinction between intellectual and emotional meaning can also be related to the debate mentioned earlier between the formalists and the expressionists. Here he also takes a compromise position and admits the existence of both intellectual and emotional meaning. 'Specifically musical' meaning posited by the formalists can be understood in Meyer's terms as intramusical intellectual meaning – the meaning of music that can be reached by intellectually grasping the relationships between the musical elements in question and the rest of the musical context.[69] On the other hand, it is not clear whether 'emotional' meaning mentioned in different versions of the expressionist view was understood by their authors as intramusical or extra-musical, although it seems more plausible that the established correspondences of musical elements and particular emotions (see Section 1.1) should be regarded as extra-musical references. Nonetheless, this distinction can help us clarify the range of possibilities that can be tested in the empirical studies. Meyer accepts the existence of both 'intramusical-emotional' meaning, conveyed by the formal musical relationships themselves, and the 'extra-musical-emotional' meaning, conveyed by musically referencing extra-musical events, emotions, etc., although he himself is mostly interested in explaining the possibility of intramusical emotional meaning.[70]

Intramusical meaning arises out of a musical event's implicit indication of a range of possible musical events to follow afterwards. These possibilities are constrained by the expectations of the listeners formed by implicit learning of rules and hierarchies in the music system. Music listeners acquire this implicit knowledge of regularities in music through frequent exposure to a particular musical style. This shapes the listeners' expectations of the subsequent musical events. As the music unfolds, the expectations are either fulfilled or disappointed, and as a result, the

---

[68] Meyer, *op. cit.*, pp. 2-3., 32-5.

[69] Meyer, *op. cit.*, pp. 39-40.

[70] Meyer, *op. cit.*, p. 35.

listeners experience relaxation or suspense.[71] Thus Meyer establishes connection between the tension-resolution patterns found in the musical structure and intramusical meaning in music. Musical expectations (which are in the basis of intramusical meaning) can be based on *intellectualizing* the uncertainty and its resolution by understanding formal musical relationships, giving rise to *intellectual* intramusical meaning, or it can be based on *feeling* the tension and relaxation, giving rise to *emotional* intramusical meaning.[72] He also believes that the disposition of the listeners and whether they were formally trained determines whether they will experience a musical event emotionally or intellectually. Formally trained listeners will wait for what they understand as the resolution of a dominant chord, while the untrained listeners, especially if they understand music primarily in emotional terms will *feel* the delay of the chord resolution as affect.[73] But even though emotional and intellectual responses to music are psychologically different, Meyer adds, they depend on the same stylistic habits, and the same musical processes give rise to and shape both types of experience.[74]

Meyer adds that the meanings observed in music are not subjective. The intramusical or extra-musical relationships, "though a product of cultural experience, are real connections existing objectively in culture. They are not arbitrary connections imposed by the capricious mind of the particular listener."[75] Both intramusical and extra-musical meanings are dependent upon learning.[76] He emphasizes that understanding music is not a matter of dispositional knowledge, for example, knowing "that in Western music of the past three hundred years (...) the dominant seventh chord creates an expectation that (...) the tonic chord will be forthcoming. The expectation must have the status of an instinctive mental and motor response, a felt

---

[71] *Ibid.*

[72] *Ibid.*

[73] Meyer, *op. cit.*, 39-40.

[74] *Ibid.*

[75] Meyer, *op. cit.*, 34.

[76] Meyer, *op. cit.*, 2.

urgency, before its meaning can be truly comprehended."[77] To illustrate this kind of ingrained habit, Meyer cites the humorous story of "the young composer who got out of his bed and ran to the piano to resolve a dominant seventh chord which someone else had left unresolved."[78]

Thus, as opposed to unified views such as formalism and expressionism, which accept only one kind and source of meaning (intramusical and intellectual versus extra-musical and emotional meaning), Meyer allows a multitude of aspects of meaning, which can be differently combined with each other, and can arise out of the same musical structures.

The next section proceeds to connect these philosophical debates concerning musical meaning with the experimental psychological research. I will present three groups of results concerning the cognitive processing of syntax and semantics in music, and show that they are relevant to the debates about musical meaning.

---

[77] Meyer, *op. cit.*, 61.

[78] *Ibid.*

2 Experimental Results Related to Meaning in Music

2.1 Formalistic Meaning in Music

The first group of results is relevant for the formalistic claim that meaning can be found in musical structure alone, and for the corresponding claim about intramusical intellectual meaning in Meyer's pluralistic account. This study shows that meaning and understanding of music are indeed significantly connected to the structural properties of music, and that the listeners make sense of the musical input by paying attention to the structure of music.

Namely, a neuroimaging study by Steinbeis and Koelsch explored the electrophysiological reactions of the brain – event-related potentials (ERPs) – to a certain type of musical stimuli.[79] This means that there are changes in the electric activity of the brain which occur each time the subjects perceive certain kind of musical stimuli, and these changes can be measured instantaneously with the use of EEG. More specifically, the study focused on a group of neurological changes that usually occur as a response to violations of syntax and semantics in language, and found similar changes in response to certain violations of musical structure.

The study aimed to test whether some of these neurological reactions may have something to do with the processing of meaning in music. Music material included in the study was designed so that it does not refer to anything outside itself – no titles, lyrics or other extra-musical signals were associated with the music material. The reactions of the participants were supposed to rely solely on the interactions between formal features of music, more specifically, on the tension-resolution patterns which are known as characteristic of the majority of compositions in Western music (see Section 1.3).[80] The authors succeeded in demonstrating that even the simplest structural features of musical structure are indeed capable of communicating meaning without referring to extra-musical events.

---

[79] Steinbeis and Koelsch, "Shared Neural Resources."

[80] Steinbeis and Koelsch *op. cit.*, 1169. See also Meyer, *op. cit.*, 60-61.

Background of the Experiment

The authors of the experiment I will present rely on the known relationship between the 'tension-resolution patterns' perceived in music and the relationships among the elements of a musical sequence (such as tones or chords) within the hierarchical organization such as the Western tonal system.[81] They cite the results of the previous research which showed that the perception of 'closeness' between two tones is correlated with the closeness of the keys the tones belong to. In addition, tones within the same key are perceived are more or less 'stable sounding' depending on their function in the key.[82] Their experimental design relies also on the fact that it was found that harmonic distance between tones or chords correlates with the perceived degree of (in)stability in music. Harmonic distance is commonly represented by the circle of fifths (See Figure 1), and this allows for an empirically measurable representation of the stability in music as well.[83] Further, it was argued in previous studies that in the basis of this perceptual phenomenon is a rule called the 'hierarchy of stability'. According to this rule, the closeness of the chord to the given harmonic context directly correlates with the perception of stability of that chord.[84] This was confirmed by the studies that found that the ratings of the tension perceived in musical events correlate with how far the event is from the 'tonal root', in both chord sequences[85] as well as musical pieces.[86] Other studies complement this by showing

---

[81] Steinbeis and Koelsch, "Shared Neural Resources," p. 1169.

[82] See Carol L. Krumhansl, "The Psychological Representation of Musical Pitch in a Tonal Context," *Cognitive Psychology*, 11 (1979):346-347.

[83] Steinbeis and Koelsch, "Shared Neural Resources," p. 1169.

[84] Jamshed Bharucha and Carol L. Krumhansl, "The Representation of Harmonic Structure in Music: Hierarchies of Stability as a Function of Context," *Cognition* 13, no. 1 (1983), pp. 63-102.

[85] Emmanuel Bigand, Richard Parncutt, and Fred Lerdahl, "Perception of Music Tension in Short Chord Sequences: the Influence of Harmonic Function, Sensory Dissonance, Horizontal Motion, and Musical Training," *Perception & Psychophysics* 58, no. 1 (1996):125-141. See also Emmanuel Bigand et al., "Effects of Global Structure and Temporal Organization on Chord Processing," *Journal of Experimental Psychology: Human Perception and Performance* 25 (1999):184-197.

that even after hearing a single chord, the subjects form expectations regarding the following events in music, and these expectations conform to the rules of harmonic distance.[87]

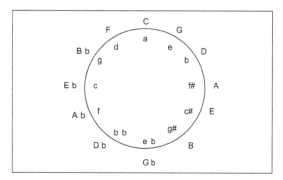

Figure 1: The circle of fifths. The outer letters represent major keys and the inner letters alongside them represent their relative minor keys. The closer the keys are in the circle, the closer they are harmonically.[88]

The Experiment

The authors of the present study attempted to add a different contribution to the experimental work already carried out. Namely, they note, the majority of research on tension-resolution patterns so far compared music with language with regard to their structural organizations, and showed that we can plausibly posit a 'syntactic analogy'

[86] See Carol L. Krumhansl, "A Perceptual Analysis of Mozart's Piano Sonata K. 282: Segmentation, Tension and Musical Ideas," *Music Perception* 13, no. 3 (1996):401-432. See also Petri Toivianinen and Carol L. Krumhansl, "Measuring and Modelling Real-Time Responses to Music: The Dynamics of Tonality Induction," *Perception* 32, no. 6 (2003):741-766., and Steinbeis et al., "The Role of Harmonic Expectancy Violations."

[87] Jamshed Bharucha and Keiko Stoeckig, "Reaction Time and Musical Expectancy: Priming of Chords," *Journal of Experimental Psychology: Human Perception and Performance* 12, no. 4 (1986): 403-410.

[88] The image was acquired from Steinbeis et al., "The Role of Harmonic Expectancy Violations." p. 1381.

between music and language.[89] The authors of the present experiment, however, wish to readdress the issue whether these formal patterns in music can also be related to meaning, i.e., to examine whether it is plausible to posit a *semantic* analogy between music and language as well.[90]

Their attempt consisted in investigating a specific neurological reaction already researched in the studies of musical expectations,[91] called the N500.[92] This reaction was observed in the previous studies as a part of the participants' response to final chords of harmonic sequences failing to fulfill harmonic expectations, for example, when the chord after the dominant chord fails to return to the tonic (which would be common in the Western music harmonic progression). The occurrence of this reaction was hitherto interpreted as reflecting (the violation of) harmonic integration, i.e., in the context of the *syntactic* analogy.[93] The reason for reassessing

---

[89] For example, in Fred Lerdahl and Ray Jackendoff, *A Generative Theory of Tonal Music*, (Cambridge (MA): MIT Press, 1983).

[90] Steinbeis and Koelsch, "Shared Neural Resources," p. 1170.

[91] Stefan Koelsch et al., "Brain Indices of Musical Processing: 'Nonmusicians' are Musical," *Journal of Cognitive Neuroscience* 12, no. 3 (2000):520-541.; See also Stefan Koelsch and Walter Siebel, "Towards a Neural Basis of Music Perception," *Trends in Cognitive Science* 9, no. 12 (2005):578-584. See also Psyche Loui et al., "Effects of Attention on the Neural Processing of Harmonic Syntax in Western Music," *Cognitive Brain Research* 25, no. 3 (2005):678-687.

[92] Names of the reactions measured in this study refer to the time and locations in the brain where the electrophysiological change is most prominent. Regarding the reactions mentioned in this study, they are most robustly measured either in the left anterior (LA), or right anterior (RA) part of the brain, while the numbers in their names such as in N400 or N500 refer to the number of milliseconds after the stimuli when the highest amplitude of the brainwave occurs. Also, the letters P and N indicate the direction of the amplitude of the measured brainwave – whether it is a positive (P) or a negative (N) amplitude. Thus, for example, the N500 is a reaction which has a negative amplitude occurring 500 milliseconds after the stimulus is presented to the subject. Similarly, LAN refers to a reaction with a negative amplitude, measured most robustly by the EEG in the left anterior region of the scalp.

[93] Koelsch et al., "Brain Indices of Musical Processing." See also Bénédicte Poulin-Charronat, Emmanuel Bigand, and Stefan Koelsch, "Processing of Musical Syntax Tonic versus

this interpretation lies in the observation of the physiological similarities between the already mentioned N500 and another reaction, named the N400, which was observed as a response to *semantically* unexpected sentences.[94] This has prompted the authors of the present study to entertain the possibility that the N500 may also have something to do with the processing of semantics in the case of music.[95] The main goal of their study was to assess this hypothesis, and possibly confirm the plausibility of a semantic analogy between music and language.

Procedure

The study involved 26 musically untrained subjects. In the experiment, the subjects were simultaneously presented with a linguistic sentence and a sequence of musical chords. The study tested the interference between processing language violations and musical expectancy violations. More specifically, it was tested whether, when the subjects hear the linguistic and harmonic violations simultaneously, there are interferences between the respective neurological reactions to these violations.[96] Examples of sentences used in the experiment are given in Table 1.

The sentence material involved 39 sentences, each composed out of 5 words. There were three versions of each sentence: a syntactically correct and semantically expected one (Table 1A), a syntactically correct and semantically unexpected one (Table 1B), and a syntactically incorrect and semantically expected one (Table 1C). The semantically 'incorrect' sentences are more accurately described as unexpected.[97]

Subdominant: An Event-Related Potential Study," *Journal of Cognitive Neuroscience* 18, no. 9 (2006):1545-1554.

[94] Steinbeis and Koelsch, "Shared Neural Resources," p. 1173.

[95] See Koelsch et al., "Brain Indices of Musical Processing," and Stefan Koelsch et al., "Processing Tonal Modulations: An ERP Study," *Journal of Cognitive Neuroscience* 15, no. 8 (2003):1149-1159.

[96] Steinbeis and Koelsch, "Shared Neural Resources," p. 1170.

[97] Steinbeis and Koelsch, "Shared Neural Resources," *ibid.*

A	B	C
Sie wuerzt das fade Essen.	Sie schaetzt das fade Essen.	Sie wuerzt den faden Essen.
She is making the dull meal.	She appreciates the bland food.	She is eating a stale food.
Sie windelt das kleine Kind.	Sie kontrolliert das kleine Kind.	Sie windelt den kleinen Kind.
She diapers the little child.	She controls the little child.	She diapers a little child.
Er zerbricht das leere Glas.	Er oefnet das leere Glas.	Er zerbricht den leeren Glas.
He breaks the empty glass.	He opens the empty glass.	He breaks a empty glass.

Table 1: Examples of sentences used in the experiment.

Column A: A syntactically correct sentence, with the semantically expected word at the end (correct sentence);

Column B: A sentence in which the word at the end is semantically unexpected (syntactically correct sentence with a semantical violation);

Column C: A sentence in which the definite article and the adjective do not correspond to the last word (syntactically incorrect sentence without a semantic violation).[98]

Musical stimuli consisted of 78 five-chord sequences. The chords were played so that each chord is presented simultaneously with one visually presented word of the sentence. Musical sequences were composed so that they contain the common Western music harmonic progressions, starting with the tonic chord, and proceeding in a way which creates high expectation of hearing the tonic chord again at the end of the sequence. The sequences were composed in two variations, either ending with the tonic chord (the expected condition), or with a Neapolitan chord (the unexpected condition).[99] In tonal harmony, the function of the Neapolitan chord is to prepare the dominant chord. Neapolitan is perceived as an unstable chord with an immediately recognizable poignant sound, which is expected to lead to the most intense chord of the sequence, usually the dominant chord. Thus, when it is instead heard after the peak, i.e., after the dominant chord, it breaks expectations of even the musically

---

[98] The examples were acquired from http://www.stefan-koelsch.de/stimulus_repository.html.

[99] *Ibid.*

untrained listeners which are merely familiar with Western music (such as the participants of this study).[100]

In the experiment, each of the three versions of the sentence was combined with each of the two versions of the musical sequence.[101] The design of the experiment is shown in Figure 2.

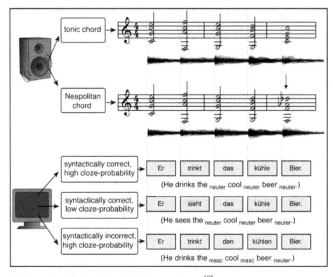

Figure 2: Examples of stimuli used in the experiment.[102]

Upper part of the image: musical stimuli – the syntactically correct (ending with the tonic chord), and the syntactically incorrect one (ending with the Neapolitan chord).

Lower part of the image: linguistic stimuli – three versions of five-word sentences.

In order to test the interference between processing of language violations and musical expectancy violations, the researchers used an 'interaction paradigm' known

[100] Barbara Tillmann, Jamshed Bharucha, and Emmanuel Bigand, "Implicit Learning of Tonality: A Self-Organizing Approach," *Psychological Review* 107, no. 4 (2000):885-913.

[101] Steinbeis and Koelsch, "Shared Neural Resources," p. 1170.

[102] The image was acquired from Steinbeis and Koelsch, "Shared Neural Resources," p. 1172.

from the previous research.[103] They also relied on an assumption suggested by earlier research that music and language have common neurological processing resources.[104] According to this assumption, music and language share resources dedicated to processing their structural aspects.[105] While they admit that it is difficult to quantify the extent of available processing, they add that there are studies which suggest that these resources are limited.[106]

The researchers first tested the reactions to the violations separately. They found that syntactically violated sentences elicit in the listeners a reaction called the "left anterior negativity" (LAN).[107] The semantically unexpected sentences elicited the already mentioned N400, which is known to be related to semantics in language from earlier research.[108] The harmonic violation elicited two distinct reactions: the N500, and the "early right anterior negativity" (ERAN).[109] These separate reactions to the different types of violations are shown in Table 2.

---

[103] Stefan Koelsch et al., "Interaction in Syntax Processing in Language and Music: an ERP Study," *Journal of Cognitive Neuroscience* 17, no. 10 (2005):1565-1577.

[104] See Aniruddh D Patel, "Language, Music, Syntax and the Brain," *Nature Neuroscience* 6, no. 7 (2003):674-681.

[105] Steinbeis and Koelsch, "Shared Neural Resources," p. 1170.

[106] Koelsch et al., "Interaction in Syntax Processing," and also L. Robert Slevc, Jason C. Rosenberg, and Aniruddh D. Patel, "Making Psycholinguistics Musical: Self-Paced Reading Time Evidence for Shared Processing of Linguistic and Musical Syntax," *Psychonomic Bulletin & Review* 16, no. 2 (2009):374-381.

[107] Steinbeis and Koelsch, "Shared Neural Resources," p. 1171.

[108] Cyma Van Petten and Marta Kutas, "Interactions Between Sentence Context and Word Frequency in Event-Related Brain Potentials," *Memory and Cognition* 18, no. 4 (1990):380-393. See also Marta Kutas and Kara D Federmeier, "Electrophysiology Reveals Semantic Memory Use in Language Comprehension," *Trends in Cognitive Sciences* 4, no. 12 (2000):463-470.

[109] Steinbeis and Koelsch, "Shared Neural Resources," p. 1171.

Type of violation in the stimuli	Neurological reaction elicited
Syntactic language violation	LAN
Semantic language violation	N400
Harmonic violation	ERAN and N500

Table 2: Types of violations and the respective neurological reactions they elicit in the listeners.

After separate measurements, they tested whether there would be interactions between these reactions when the subjects are presented with linguistic sentences and musical sequences simultaneously. The study aimed to reveal whether either of the two neurological reactions to harmonic violations (ERAN and N500) reflects the processing of semantics in music.[110] As already mentioned, the background assumption adopted in this study was that music and language share the (limited) resources dedicated to processing of their structural aspects. When the subject is presented simultaneously with the harmonic and linguistic violation, there are three possible outcomes concerning the behavior of either ERAN or N500:

1) The reaction is reduced only when it occurs simultaneously with the *semantic* linguistic violation. This would suggest that the reaction itself also reflects semantic processes related to the harmonic violations, since it shares the limited resources with semantic processing of language input.[111]

2) The reaction is modulated only when occurring simultaneously with the *syntactic* linguistic violation. This would suggest that it also reflects syntactic processes of the harmonic violations, since it is the syntactic processing resources that are shared.[112]

3) The reaction is modulated when it occurs simultaneously with either semantic or syntactic language violation. This would suggest that the reaction might reflect more *general* memory demands (resulting from any kind of unexpected event).[113]

---

[110] *Ibid.*

[111] Steinbeis and Koelsch, "Shared Neural Resources," p. 1170.

[112] *Ibid.*

Since in the previous research the function of the reaction named ERAN was associated with the syntactic processes,[114] the authors of this experiment hypothesized that ERAN will be reduced only when coinciding with the syntactic violations of sentences (option 2).[115] More importantly, they were interested in the behavior of the N500 because, as already mentioned, it possesses physiological similarities with the N400 which is already associated with semantic processing. Along with the hypothesis concerning the behavior of ERAN, the other main hypothesis was that N500 will be modulated only when occurring simultaneously with the semantic violation of language (i.e. that it would behave according to option 1).[116]

Results

The results confirmed both hypotheses. The interference occurred exclusively, as hypothesized, between ERAN and the syntactic violations on one hand, and between N500 and the semantic violations on the other hand. ERAN was significantly modulated by the syntactic violation, and remained unaffected by the semantic violation (confirming the option 2). Conversely, N500 was only significantly modulated only by the semantic violation, and remained unaffected by the syntactic violation (confirming the option 1). The interference between the neurological reactions is shown in Figure 3. This is taken to indicate that ERAN reflects syntactic, and N500 semantic processes related to the harmonic violations of musical sequences, and that neither of them seems to be associated with the more general processes related to attention or working memory (because they were reduced for only one type of language material violation), thus refuting option 3 for both reactions.[117] The

---

[113] *Ibid.* The researchers did not consider the fourth option, namely, that there would be no change in the reaction. Nonetheless, this option did not occur in the experiment, and therefore does not need further consideration.

[114] See Koelsch et al., "Interaction in Syntax Processing."

[115] Steinbeis and Koelsch, "Shared Neural Resources," p. 1170.

[116] *Ibid.*, p. 1173.

[117] *Ibid.*, p. 1171-2.

authors further note that, since the semantic unexpectedness in the language material was very mild, the results concerning the behavior of the N500 reaction are even more significant for positing the semantic analogy between music and language.[118]

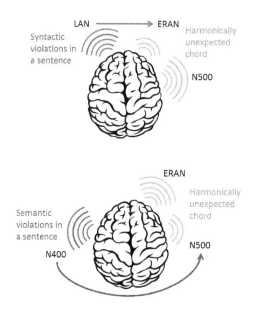

Figure 3: Illustration of the interference between the responses to the simultaneously presented violations in linguistic and musical material. When the violation of musical material is presented simultaneously with a syntactic violation of a sentence, the ERAN response becomes reduced. When the musical violation is presented with a semantic violation of a sentence, only N500 is reduced.

The results also confirm the background assumption that music and language share the neural resources dedicated to the processing of their structural aspects, and that these resources are indeed limited – since the reactions tended to get reduced when occurring simultaneously. If the resources were unlimited, reactions to both linguistic and harmonic violations might have fully developed, and the experiment could not allow determining whether the resources are indeed shared, whether there are

---

[118] Steinbeis and Koelsch, "Shared Neural Resources," p. 1174.

interactions occurring between different neurological reactions, and which reaction reflects which aspect (syntactic or semantic) of processing.

The researchers additionally note that, while it has already been shown that music and language share neural resources on the syntactic level,[119] the data obtained in this experiment are the first to show that the two domains (music and language) also share neural resources on a *semantic* level.[120] This suggests that it is plausible to posit not only a syntactic, but also a semantic analogy between music and language.

Implications of the Results

Relationship Between Structure and Meaning

The results of the present study show evidence of an interaction between the processing of the harmonic structure and the processing of the semantic aspect of language. This can be taken to indicate that paying attention to the structure in music leads to semantic processing. In other words, the listeners seem to make sense of music through the features of its structure. This study, thus, provides evidence that the formal properties of music alone can be perceived as meaningful even by musically untrained subjects. This also indicates that musical form alone can convey meaning even if it does not refer to, or associate the listeners with other meaningful objects or extra-musical events.

---

[119] Aniruddh D Patel et al., "Processing Syntactic Relations in Language and Music: An Event-Related Potential Study," *Journal of Cognitive Neuroscience* 10, no. 6 (1998):717-733. See also Patel, "Language, Music, Syntax and the Brain," and Koelsch et al., "Interaction in Syntax Processing in Language and Music."

[120] Steinbeis and Koelsch, "Shared Neural Resources," p. 1175.

The Role of Musical Expectations

These results seem to support Meyer's view that meaning in music is not necessarily tied to moods or emotions, and that it can arise out of familiarity of the listeners with the regularities in music, implicitly acquired through frequent exposure to music or a particular style (see Section 1.3).[121] Even though the participants were not musically trained, their reactions to the sequence endings atypical for Western music show that they did have implicit expectations of how the sequences would end. The meaning they found in the sequences can be described in Meyer's terms as intramusical intellectual meaning.

Formalistic meaning

These results also seem to support the formalist claim of the existence of specifically musical meaning, in that musical structures themselves are perceived as meaningful (see Section 1.1). This is in accord with the formalists' postulation of the existence of purely musical ideas. In other words, the musical sequences presented in the experiment seemed to be developing the musical idea in one direction (toward the tonic chord at the end), and then switched to an atypical chord, leading to a slight surprise reaction in the listeners, similar to the reactions to the semantically unexpected sentences. In addition, the formalistic claim that musical form is the content of a musical piece seem compatible with the finding that the same change in musical form is reflected on the neural indicators of both syntactic and semantic processing. This twofold reaction to the same violation might be interpreted as registering a violation of both the form and the content of the musical sequence.

---

[121] See also Tillmann et al., "Implicit Learning of Tonality."

Semantic Analogy Between Music and Language

Since the results supported the experimenters' postulation of a semantic analogy between music and language (in addition to the already discussed and researched syntactic one), it seems natural to follow the analogy further, and ask which aspect of music constitutes its semantics, and which constitutes its syntax. Since the analogy posits the existence of two separate aspects (supported by two separate neurological reactions for processing each aspect), how is this distinction reflected in the music itself? The question is especially intriguing due to the fact that the structural harmonic violation in this experiment seems to have violated both syntax and semantics – judging by the two separate processing reactions.

The authors of the experiment did not offer any suggestions regarding this question. I propose a distinction that might fit the syntax-semantics analogy with language, yet still capture the specific manner in which music operates, regardless of its similarities with language.

What are Musical Syntax and Semantics

Musical syntax can be understood as the group of rules defining certain musical style or genre. These rules can be more or less specific, depending on whether they apply to e.g. Western music in general, or to a specific genre within that style, or even more specific if they define a certain subgenre. For example, although classical music, jazz, and pop music all adhere to certain very general rules of Western music (similar harmonic structure, phrases ending with cadences, etc.), each of them adheres to their own, more specific set of rules which makes them recognizable as those specific genres. The rules which define a certain genre constitute the syntax of music belonging to that genre. The listeners internalize these rules as they become familiar with the music of that genre, either explicitly, through training and theoretical knowledge, or implicitly, through frequent exposure to such music. When the defining rules of the genre are violated, the violations can be heard as a syntactic mistake within the genre, or sometimes as entering a different genre. If the violations of a given syntax are sufficiently consistent or skillfully performed, they tend to constitute rules of an alternative syntax. Excerpts of atonal music, for example, if played randomly within the context of tonal music, will most probably be heard as mistakenly breaking the syntactic rules of tonal music. However, if the violations are consistent enough, they may cue the listeners to hear these violations as part of an alternative, atonal syntax.

Musical semantics, on the other hand, can be understood as the aspect of music which consists in the specific musical ideas that the composer wished to express – within a given style or genre. These ideas can be more or less interesting, original, complex or simple. They consist in the composer (more or less skillfully) manipulating the music material within the rules of a given style or genre. For example, sometimes the composer can perfectly adhere to the rules of a genre, albeit the musical ideas presented in the work are dull. Conversely, the composer can violate the syntax of a style (e.g. briefly adhere to the rules of a different style), in order to further develop the musical idea and make it more interesting.

Musical Syntax and Semantics in the Experiment

Furthermore, just like in language, sometimes the same act in a musical sequence can violate both syntax and semantics simultaneously (e.g. if the last word of the sentence "She is making the dull meal" was omitted, the sentence would both lose its meaning and become syntactically incorrect). I believe it is exactly what was performed in the present experiment. Namely, no matter how short the musical sequence (it consisted of only five chords), the appearance of the Neapolitan chord at the end of the phrase after the dominant chord violated both the musical idea that the listeners might have expected to develop in the sequence, as well as the rules of the style of Western music.

My proposition also fits the formalistic idea that the content of music lies in the form itself (see Section 1.2). Musical ideas are manifested in the formal structure, and this formal structure possesses a syntactic and a semantic level. That is what enables the same structural violation (such as the one performed in the experiment) to violate both levels at once, and elicit two separate neurological reactions (ERAN and N500) to the violation of each level.

2.2 Emotional Meaning in Music

The second group of results introduces another possibility into the debate on meaning in music. Steinbeis, Koelsch and Sloboda designed an experiment which should directly test the role of the tension-resolution patterns in music in creating emotional responses in the listeners.[122]

This study is relevant for Meyer's claim that properties of musical structure alone (without the help of referential or extra-musical signs) can generate emotional meaning (see Section 1.3). The results obtained could also be relevant for the expressionists, in case their accounts of emotional meaning in music did not rely exclusively on the referential correspondences between musical elements and particular emotions (see Section 1.1). Unfortunately, they did not explicitly refer to this distinction of the sources of the emotional meaning in music, and thus it is not clear how relevant these results are for those accounts.

Background of the Experiment

The design of the present experiment relies on the similar background as the previous experiment on specifically musical meaning (Section 2.1). It also relies on the generally acknowledged claim that cognitive processes take part in the emergence of emotional processes, and that among cognitive processes in general, *expectations* are especially important, since they lead the subjects to feelings of satisfaction, disappointment, surprise, etc. [123] In particular, the authors of this study focused on

---

[122] Steinbeis et al., "The Role of Harmonic Expectancy Violations."

[123] See Nico H. Frijda, "The Place of Appraisal in Emotion," *Cognition and Emotion* 7, no. 3-4 (1993):357-387. See also Craig A. Smith and Richard S. Lazarus, "Appraisal Components,

harmonic expectations, and their role in generating emotional responses. Even though musical expectations in general have been studied for melody,[124] rhythm,[125] and harmony,[126] this study focused on harmony only, because harmony is the aspect of music which can most conveniently be quantified by means of the circle of fifths (See Figure 1, and also see Section 2.1).[127]

Expectations and Harmonic Distance

Harmonic expectations are known to be related to the principles of harmonic distance underlying Western music, meaning that chords distant from the tonal root are usually less expected than chords closer to the root.[128] For example, if the section of the musical piece is in the key of C (meaning that C note is the root), it is expected to hear the G or D chords, but it is very unexpected to hear G flat chord (see Figure 1). Importantly, having these expectations does not require conscious knowledge of the principles of harmonic distance. They can occur by unconscious processing of

---

Core Relational Themes, and the Emotions," *Cognition and Emotion* 7, no. 3-4 (1993):233-269.

[124] Mari Jones, Marilyn Boltz, and Gary R. Kidd, "Controlled Attending as a Function of Melodic and Temporal Context," *Perception and Psychophysics* 32, no. 3 (1982): 211-218.

[125] Marilyn G. Boltz, "The Generation of Temporal and Melodic Expectancies During Musical Listening," *Perception and Psychophysics* 53, no. 6 (1993): 585-600. Also see Eugene Narmour, *The Analysis and Cognition of Basic Melodic Structures* (Chicago: University of Chicago Press, 1990).

[126] Mark A. Schmuckler, "Expectation in Music: Investigation of Melodic and Harmonic Processes," *Music Perception*, 7, no. 2 (1989): 109-150. See also Bharucha and Stoeckig, "Reaction Time and Musical Expectancy."

[127] Steinbeis et al., "The Role of Harmonic Expectancy Violations," p. 1380.

[128] Tillmann et al., "Implicit Learning of Tonality." See also Koelsch et al., "Brain Indices of Musical Processing."

harmonic relations,[129] which is the result of implicitly learning harmonic principles through repeated exposure to Western music (see Sections 1.3 and 2.1). In other words, familiarity with certain musical style has a more important role in forming harmonic expectations than any theoretical knowledge.[130] The connection between expectations and harmonic distance was empirically supported in one previous study which showed that, after hearing only one chord, the participants have expectations concerning how distant the next chord will be.[131]

Harmonic Distance and Tension

Harmonic distance, on the other hand, was related to the musical 'tension' perceived by the listeners. Chords far away from the tonal root (e.g. G flat in the key of C) tend to be perceived as more tense than chords closer to the root (such as, say, F, G, D, etc.). This connection between tension and distance was empirically supported in studies with chord sequences,[132] and in studies using real music,[133] which showed that harmonic distance between two keys correlates to the tension the listeners perceive in music.[134]

---

[129] Emmanuel Bigand et al., "The Effect of Harmonic Context on Phoneme Monitoring in Vocal Music," *Cognition* 81, no. 1 (2001): B11-B20.

[130] Steinbeis et al., "The Role of Harmonic Expectancy Violations," p. 1380.

[131] Bharucha and Stoeckig, "Reaction Time and Musical Expectancy."

[132] Emmanuel Bigand et al., "Effect of Global Structure and Temporal Organisation on Chord Processing," *Journal of Experimental Psychology: Human Perception and Performance* 2 (1999): 184-197. See also Bigand et al., "Perception of Music Tension in Short Chord Sequences."

[133] Toiviainen and Krumhansl, "Measuring and Modelling Real-Time Responses to Music." See also Krumhansl, "A Perceptual Analysis of Mozart's Piano Sonata," and Carol L. Krumhansl, "Music: A Link Between Cognition and Emotion," *Current Directions in Psychological Science*, 11, no. 2 (2002): 45-50.

[134] Steinbeis et al., "The Role of Harmonic Expectancy Violations," p. 1381.

Tension and Emotions

Another connection, also established in previous research is between tension and emotions in music. In one study on the expressive properties of dance and music, participants were asked to rate, first, the amount of tension they perceived in music, and then the strength of the 'expressed emotion'. The results showed high correlations between these ratings both in regard to whole musical pieces and on the 'moment to moment' level.[135] The authors of the following experiment consider this finding as significant. They believe that the tension perceived in music perhaps represents a connecting link between musical expectations and emotions felt by the listeners. They posit musical tension as a 'connecting concept', which could help us understand "what it is about the unexpected that makes it emotional."[136]

The Experiment

The experiment I will present in this section relies on the correlations found between, first, musical (un)expectedness and harmonic distance, second, harmonic distance and tension, and finally tension and felt emotions. Based on this multiply mediated link between musical expectations and emotions, the authors of the following study wanted also to test whether there might also be a direct link between these two phenomena. Their experiment was designed to directly test the correlation between musical unexpectedness and emotional responses. The authors searched for this correlation by comparing emotional responses in the listeners (by measuring subjective ratings and physiological indicators) with musical passages with different degrees of harmonic unexpectedness.[137]

---

[135] Carol L. Krumhansl and Diana Lynn Schenck, "Can Dance Reflect the Structural and Expressive Qualities of Music? A Perceptual Experiment on Balanchine's Choreography of Mozart's Divertimento No. 15," *Musicae Scientiae* 1 (1997): 63-85.

[136] Steinbeis et al., "The Role of Harmonic Expectancy Violations," p. 1380.

[137] *Ibid.*

Procedure

The study involved 24 participants, twelve of which were musically trained, with averagely 13.8 years of musical education. The other twelve did not have any musical training beyond the one routinely provided at school.[138]

As stimuli, the authors used excerpts from six compositions by J. S. Bach. Each excerpt had three versions. The first was the original Bach's version, which incorporated an unexpected event, usually occurring in the cadence. The other two were electronically manipulated versions of the original excerpt, so that in the place of the unexpected event, the participants hear either a more expected event, or an even more *un*expected event.[139] The unexpectedness of the event by which these versions differed was determined by the authors of the study, according to their 'musical intuition', which they afterwards substantiated by measuring the distance of the event (the 'target') from the tonic root, through the use of the circle of fifths.[140] The more expected manipulation of the excerpt usually contained a return to the tonic at the end, while the very unexpected one contained a Neapolitan chord instead of the tonic.[141] Examples of these three versions of the sequence differing in expectedness are shown in Figure 4.

---

[138] *Ibid.*, p. 1383.

[139] *Ibid.*

[140] *Ibid.*

[141] For an explanation of the atypicality of the Neapolitan chord occurring after the dominant chord, see Section 2.1.

Figure 4: Examples of musical sequences used in the study.[142]

The sequence starts in D-major. After passing through the subdominant and dominant chords (a common progression in Western music), the ending chord is:

A) b-minor – the parallel minor of D-major. This is the slightly unexpected ending which appears in the original sequence;

B) D-major – the tonic chord. Returning to the tonic is the most expected ending of such a sequence, and it is thus the more expected version than the original;

C) E flat-major – the Neapolitan chord. The appearance of the Neapolitan chord after the dominant is highly atypical for Western music, and this sequence ends in a far more unexpected way than the original.

In the experiment, the researchers searched for both behavioral and physiological evidence of the connection between the unexpectedness of the final chord in the sequence and the emotional reaction of the subjects.

In the behavioral part of the experiment, three measures were recorded:

(a) the intensity of felt emotion during the musical sequence;

(b) the intensity of the tension they perceived in music; and

(c) the 'overall intensity' of emotional response rated at the end of each sequence.

---

[142] The image was acquired from Steinbeis et al., "The Role of Harmonic Expectancy Violations," p. 1384.

The subjects gave self-reports on these three subjective measures, by rating each measure on the continuous scale from 0 to 100 for measures (a) and (b), and from 1 to 10 for measure (c).[143]

In the physiological part of the experiment, the researchers recorded several physiological measures while the subjects were listening to the musical sequences: electrodermal activity (EDA), the inter-heartbeat interval (IBI), and the changes in the electrophysiological activity of the brain (measured in event-related potentials, or ERPs).[144] The relevance of the physiological measures will be explained bellow.

Electrodermal activity (EDA) indicates the variation of the electrical properties of the skin as a result of sweat secretion. In other words, EDA refers to the changes in 'skin conductance levels'. Sweating is controlled by the sympathetic nervous system, and the rise of skin conductance level resulting from the sweating is an indication of psychological or physiological *arousal*.[145]

Inter-heartbeat interval (IBI) refers to the time interval between individual beats of the mammalian heart, and it is generally measured in units of milliseconds. In healthy heart function, this interval is irregular – it varies from beat to beat. In other words, the intervals between heart beats are normally of different lengths. For example, the interval between the successive heartbeats can be 0.86 seconds between one pair of succeeding heartbeats and 1.34 seconds between another pair of beats. This is colloquially called "healthy irregularity".[146] When a series of these intervals is calculated, it gives a measure called heart rate variability (HRV). Higher variability indicates higher irregularity between heartbeat intervals. Lower variability (it can reach as low as 0) indicates more regular inter-heartbeat interval. While generally

---

[143] Steinbeis et al., "The Role of Harmonic Expectancy Violations," p. 1384.

[144] *Ibid.*, p. 1385.

[145] Mathias Benedeka and Christian Kaernbach, "A Continuous Measure of Phasic Electrodermal Activity," *Journal of Neuroscience Methods* 190, no.1 (2010): 80-91.

[146] Marjolein Van Der Zwaag, Joyce Westerink, and Egon L. van den Broek, "Emotional and Psychophysiological Responses to Tempo, Mode, and Percussiveness," *Musicae Scientiae* 15, no. 2 (2011): 250-269.

these measures can indicate certain health conditions, when measured in individual persons across a short time-span and compared, they can reveal information about their *emotional* states. Heart rate variability is known to be higher during pleasant experiences, related to relaxation or other non-stressful or pleasant situations, while, conversely, during tense and unpleasant states, the variability decreases, indicating that heartbeats follow a stricter pattern.[147]

The empirical literature on emotions as well showed that these two measures (EDA and IBI) correlate with the valence and the arousal dimension of the emotional experience.[148] Arousal (measured by the electrodermal activity) indicates the degree of emotional intensity: higher arousal means higher intensity of a felt emotion. Valence (measured by the heart rate variability) refers to the perceived (un)pleasantness of the stimulus. Higher variability is correlated with higher pleasantness, and vice versa. By recording changes in these two physiological measures, the authors of the experiment searched for empirical evidence related to the two primary dimensions of emotional response.[149]

Hypotheses

The authors of the present experiment combined several measures in order to obtain a 'more integrated analysis'. They formulated their hypotheses in regard to each measure. They predicted that harmonic unexpectedness will correlate with:

(a) the subjective ratings of emotional intensity during listening;

(b) the subjective ratings of the tension perceived in the sequences;

(c) the subjective ratings of the overall emotional intensity after the sequences;

(d) an increase in heart rate variability and electrodermal activity;

---

[147] *Ibid.*

[148] Margaret M. Bradley and Peter J. Lang, "Affective Reactions to Acoustic Stimuli," *Psychophysiology*, 37, (2000): 204-215. See also Margaret M. Bradley, Peter J. Lang, and Bruce N. Cuthbert, "Emotion, Novelty, and the Startle Reflex: Habituation in Humans," *Behavioural Neuroscience*, 107, (1993): 970-980.

[149] Steinbeis et al., "The Role of Harmonic Expectancy Violations," p. 1382.

(e) the increase of the amplitude of the neurological reaction ('early right anterior negativity', or ERAN)[150] which reflects the processing of the unexpected stimuli;

The authors of the study also predicted that (f) the musically trained subjects will show stronger reactions in both behavioral and physiological measures than untrained subjects. They based this prediction on the assumption that musically trained subjects have internalized the rules of Western music to a higher degree, "and should therefore be more sensitive to their violations."[151]

Results

Behavioral results

The results of the behavioral part of the study showed that local emotionality judgments (a), recorded continuously during the listening of the musical pieces, showed no increase with the increase of harmonic unexpectedness. On the other hand, local tension judgments (b), also recorded continuously, correlated with unexpectedness, in a way that the greatest increase in tension followed the most unexpected harmony. The overall emotional impact ratings (c) given at the end of each musical sequence also correlated with musical unexpectedness, with a significant difference between all three conditions, in the same way as for the tension judgments (expected < unexpected < very unexpected). The harmonic expectancy violations consisted of only one chord, and the authors of the study note that "it is therefore particularly striking that perceived tension and the overall emotional impact of a musical piece" can be influenced by "as little as one specific musical event."[152]

In summary, significant effects of harmonic unexpectedness were found for local tension and overall emotional response report, and thus hypotheses (b) and (c) were confirmed, while hypothesis (a) regarding local emotional response was refuted.

---

[150] For a detailed explanation of the role of ERAN in the processing of musical structure, see Section 2.1.

[151] Steinbeis et al., "The Role of Harmonic Expectancy Violations," p. 1383.

[152] *Ibid.*, p. 1390.

49

Physiological results

The physiological results complement the subjective reports of the participants. Similarly to the judgments on local tension perceived in the music, the electrodermal activity (EDA) increased with the increase of harmonic unexpectedness. This suggests that arousal correlated with harmonic unexpectedness. More specifically, this measure increased significantly for the unexpected (original) versions in comparison to the expected versions, and increased the most for very unexpected harmonies.[153]

The inter-heartbeat interval (IBI), however, did not increase with the unexpectedness. Since inter-heartbeat interval is an indicator of valence (pleasantness or unpleasantness) of the subject's experience, this lack of significant changes indicates that harmonic unexpectedness may not be related with the valence dimension of an emotional response, but instead solely with the degree of arousal.[154]

The results of the EEG showed that the unexpected (original) chord elicited a distinct neurological reaction related to the structural violations of auditory input (ERAN), as hypothesized in (e). This means that the participants registered the unexpected musical event, at least unconsciously. More importantly, the amplitude of this measure was even larger for the very unexpected chord (Neapolitan Sixth). The finding that the amplitude was larger for the very unexpected than for the merely unexpected chord supports the assumption that such neurological response is sensitive to the *degree* of harmonic unexpectedness, since the higher music-syntactic irregularity (in the very unexpected version) evoked a larger amplitude than the milder irregularity (in the original version).[155]

Interestingly, even though the measures significant for the emotional response did not differ in musicians and non-musicians, the neurological reactions occurred slightly earlier in musicians, and were accompanied by certain additional

---

[153] *Ibid.*, p. 1386.

[154] *Ibid.*

[155] *Ibid.*

components.[156] This indicates that musicians processed the unexpected chords more rapidly, or merely differently, but in any case, these differences did not lead to the different emotional responses. This was contrary to the part of the hypothesis (f) that claimed that musicians will have stronger emotional responses because they are more familiar with the rules of Western music.

In summary, the physiological results only partly confirm hypothesis (d) by establishing a correlation between electrodermal activity (EDA, which indicates emotional arousal level) and harmonic unexpectedness. The correlation between valence dimension of emotion was not found. Hypothesis (e) regarding the correlation between neurological reactions characteristic for the processing of structural violations and harmonic unexpectedness was also confirmed by the results. The last hypothesis (f), proposing stronger reactions in musicians to the irregular events was only confirmed for neurological processing, but not for the emotional arousal and subjective ratings.

Implications of the Results

Musical Expectations and Emotional Responses

Even though a significant correlation between the valence dimension of emotions (indicated by the inter-heartbeat interval or IBI) and harmonic unexpectedness was not observed, the correlation of unexpectedness with the emotional arousal (indicated by the increased electrodermal activity or EDA, the subjective ratings of tension, and of overall emotional response) provides some evidence in support of the role of the musical structure and musical expectations in the emotional experience of the listeners. These results, thus, establish the relationship the authors hoped for, namely,

---

[156] Certain unhypothesized neurological reactions were elicited, and they differed in musicians and non-musicians, but they are not pertinent to the topic of this chapter. For more information on these reactions, see Steinbeis et al., "The Role of Harmonic Expectancy Violations," pp. 1388-90. For more discussion on neurocognitive and other differences between musically trained and untrained subjects, see Chapter II.

the relationship between harmonic expectancies and emotional responses, which was missing in the empirical literature on music and the emotions.

The direct proportion of the amplitude of the neurological reaction (ERAN) with the other measures supports the notion that it was the harmonic irregularity that was 'responsible' for the emotional response, since it confirms that the irregularities were processed, even if the participants were not conscious of them.

The authors of the study took these findings to suggest the existence of a causal link, starting with the perception of tension (caused by harmonic unexpectedness) which induces an increase in arousal, and the arousal finally predisposes the subjects to an increase in an overall emotional response.[157]

The lack of differences between musically trained and untrained subjects in both behavioral and physiological indicators of an emotional response reveals that this causal chain, as well as the intensity of the emotional response to music do not depend on the degree of expertise. In addition, the authors of the study emphasize that the emotional influence on the subjects was evoked by musical sequences which were "synthesized electronically and possessed none of the other expressive attributes normally inherent to human performance (e.g., variations in tempo and loudness)."[158] They conclude that this suggests that the emotional effects of musical structure alone are robust.[159]

Support for Meyer's Account

These results can be taken to support Meyer's claim that it is possible for the properties of the musical structure itself to have emotional meaning for the listeners, even without referencing emotions with extra-musical signs (such as titles, etc.), or the (also extra-musical) correspondences between particular musical elements and

---

[157] Steinbeis et al., "The Role of Harmonic Expectancy Violations," p. 1390.

[158] *Ibid.*

[159] *Ibid.*

particular emotions. In other words, this study supports Meyer's notion of intramusical emotional meaning, since it is shown that music can have an emotional impact solely through the fulfillment or suspension of specifically musical expectations (see Section 1.3).

Limitations (and Potential for the Expressionists)

The lack of local emotionality changes suggests that harmonic unexpectedness only predisposes the listeners to an increase in the general emotional arousal (indicated by the ratings of the overall emotional intensity), which further leads to a stronger experience of the particular emotion correlated with the musical piece. Since the structural changes affected only one main dimension of emotion (the arousal), and did not affect the valence of the emotional experience, there is still room for interpretation of the relevance of these results for the issue of emotional meaning in music.

Suggestions for Further Research

The limitations of this study leave some potential for the expressionists, who can claim that the correspondences that they posit between musical elements and particular emotions are needed to supplement the structural events with the valence dimension of emotions. In other words, the expressionists could claim that the tension-resolution patterns account only for the general arousal of the listener, while the correspondences are what turns this general arousal into a more specific emotional experience (see Section 1.1 for details on the expressionist view). Such correspondences can be tested empirically.

Similarly, more studies need to be conducted that focus on the physiological markers of different emotions experienced as a result of different structural features. One of the rare studies which systematically examined a number of physiological measures related to emotional processing found that sad musical sequences had the highest impact on the cardiac and the electrodermal system, while happy sequences influenced the respiratory system, and fearful sequences affected mainly the cardiovascular one, thereby indicating that different emotional character of music may evoke emotions with different physiological characteristics.[160] Their results, along with the results of the present study, suggest the possible direction for further empirical exploration of the relationship between musical structure, meaning and the emotions, in which different emotional characteristics of musical structure could be brought into a relation with the different emotions.

2.3 Conceptual Meaning in Music

The third group of results provides some surprising insights for the debate on meaning in music. Instead of lending support for one or the other kind of meaning already postulated by the philosophers, it introduces new possibilities regarding the scope of musical meaning. While the philosophers debated on the primacy of the emotional versus specifically musical meaning, the following study presents an option that was not entertained by the philosophers, namely, that musical structure might possess conceptual meaning, independently of extra-musical signals such as titles, lyrics or programs, and also not mediated by the emotional meaning.[161]

Both extreme sides of the philosophical debate on meaning – the formalists and the expressionists – agreed that music cannot convey this kind of conceptual content (see Sections 1.1 and 1.2). Additionally, even though he was more permissive to the various types of meaning than other theoreticians, Meyer did not mention the possibility of extra-musical conceptual meaning either (see Section 1.3).

The following study provides evidence for the relationship between musical structures and concepts denied by the philosophers, and therefore refutes one of the few points of (at least implicit) agreement between the debating parties.

---

[160] Carol L. Krumhansl, "An Exploratory Study of Musical Emotions and Psychophysiology," *Canadian Journal of Experimental Psychology* 51, no. 4 (1997): 336-352.

[161] Koelsch et al., "Music, Language and Meaning."

Background of the Experiment

Priming

The method used in the following study involved "priming" – a technique commonly used in experimental psychology, whereby exposure of the subject to one stimulus (called the 'prime') influences (affects the speed of) a response to the subsequent stimulus (usually called the 'target'). Positive priming is priming that speeds up processing of the target stimulus. This effect on the processing speed is called the "priming effect." There are several competing accounts of the exact underlying mechanisms of the priming effect,[162] however, we do not need to go into details of those accounts. The authors of the following study rely only on the empirical evidence for the existence of such effect, regardless of its underlying mechanisms. More specifically, they rely on the existence of the *semantic* priming effect, where the prime and the target stimulus are semantically related. In semantic priming, processing of the target input is facilitated by the preceding input if the two inputs are semantically related. For example, the sentence "She sings a song" facilitates processing of the semantically related word 'music', while it does not facilitate processing of the semantically unrelated word 'sock'.[163] This effect can be observed in the behavioral reactions, by measuring the speed of the reactions of the participants, e.g. how fast they perform tasks related to the target stimuli.

The semantic effect can also be observed in the physiological reactions. If the EEG measurements are conducted during the priming experiments, they show a specific change in the electrophysiological activity of the brain. This change in activity, which is considered the physiological indicator of semantic priming is named the 'N400' amplitude of the brainwave.[164] For example, when a word (the target) is preceded by certain semantic context (the prime), the amplitude of the N400

---

[162] Daniel Reisberg, *Cognition: Exploring the Science of the Mind*, (New York: W. W. Norton & Company, Inc., 2007), pp. 255, 517.

[163] Examples taken from Koelsch et al., "Music, Language and Meaning," p. 302.

[164] The name 'N400' refers to the highest amplitude of the brainwave with a negative (N) direction, occurring around 400ms after the stimulus onset. For a more detailed explanation of this type of electrophysiological reactions, see Section 2.1, fn 81.

brainwave is "inversely related to the degree of semantic fit between the word and its preceding semantic context."[165] In other words, the more semantically related the word is to its context, the lower the N400 amplitude, and vice versa.

The Experiment

The stimuli used in semantic priming experiments (e.g. words, sentences, morphemes, etc.) are usually taken from the linguistic domain. This study, however, expanded the domain to both linguistic and musical stimuli, in order to test whether the semantic effect might occur between the two domains. As the authors note, while intuitively it does seem plausible that certain passages of Beethoven's symphonies would prime the meaning of the word 'hero', rather than the meaning of the word 'flea', no studies were conducted to experimentally test such a relationship.[166] If semantic relationships were observed between musical and linguistic stimuli, the authors hypothesize, it might indicate that music can transfer at least some conceptual content. The ultimate goal of their study, thus, was to test whether music can convey conceptual content, in particular, whether it can convey particular concepts to the listeners.[167]

Procedure

In order to test this hypothesis, the authors conducted a classical semantic priming experiment, with the addition of musical excerpts as primes. More specifically, the experiment involved two kinds of primes: musical primes (musical excerpts), and linguistic primes (sentences). The target stimuli were single words. The experiment was designed to test the semantic effect between each group of primes and the target words.

---

[165] Koelsch et al., "Music, Language and Meaning," p. 302.

[166] *Ibid.*

[167] *Ibid.*

The pre-experiment

In order to gain a preliminary assessment of the semantic relations between the primes and the targets, a pre-experiment was conducted, in which a large group of subjects[168] rated the 'semantic fit' between numerous potential primes and target words, for both linguistic and musical primes. In other words, the subjects judged whether the stimuli were semantically close or not. They were asked to rate the degree of semantic fit between the primes and the target words on an 11-point scale, ranging from -5 (semantically strongly unrelated) to +5 (semantically strongly related). The stimuli with non-significant ratings were discarded from the main experiment.[169]

The main experiment

In the main experiment, the target words were 44 nouns, half of which were abstract words, while the other half were concrete, e.g., 'wideness', 'narrowness', 'needle', 'cellar', 'stairs', 'river', 'king', 'illusion'.[170] Some of these examples, along with the musical pieces used as stimuli are shown in Table 3.

The musical primes were chosen based on several different principles. One third of them was chosen based on the self-reports of the composers. For example, the excerpt of Schönberg's String Terzett in which he claimed to had portrayed the stitches during his heart attack was used as the semantically related prime for the word 'needle'. Another group of musical stimuli was chosen based on musicological terminology. For instance, a sequence in which the notes are close together (extending in a narrow pitch range) was used as prime for the word 'narrowness'. Similarly, a sequence in which the notes are wide apart (extending in a wide pitch range) was the prime stimuli for the word 'wideness'. As an instance of another group of musical primes, the researchers mention the sequence from Stravinsky which can be said to sound fervent, and the word 'fervent' is semantically related to the target word 'red'. For the concrete words, the authors chose musical primes which resemble the extra-

---

[168] None of these subjects participated in any other part of the experiment.

[169] Koelsch et al., "Music, Language and Meaning," p. 306.

[170] *Ibid.*, p. 302-3.

musical sounds (such as the prime for 'bird') or properties (low tones were primes for 'basement', while ascending tonal steps were primes for 'staircase').[171]

		Related	Unrelated
Heikki Valpola, (*1946) Clowns The sad clown		limitedness	wideness
Richard Strauss, (1864-1949) Salome, Op 54 Tanz der sieben Schleier (Dance of the Seven Veils)		wideness	limitedness
Arnold Schönberg, (1874-1951) String Trio, Op 45		needle	river
J. S. Bach, (1685-1750) Das wohltemperierte Klavier (The Well-Tempered Clavier), BWV 846-869 Prelude in C minor		river	needle
Dimitri Schostakowitsch, (1906-1975) Symphony No 5, Op 47 IV. Allegro non troppo		men	women
Ottorino Repighi, (1879-1936) La boutique fantasque, ballet after Rossini V. Cancan		women	men
Sergej Prokofiev, (1891-1953) Scythian Suite, Op 20 III. Night		glass	circle

Table 3: Examples of the compositions and target words used in the study.[172]

As already noted, half of the linguistic primes were semantically related to the target words, e.g., the sentence "The gaze wandered into the distance" was the semantically related prime for the target word "wideness", while the sentence "The manacles allow only little movement" was the semantically unrelated prime to the same target word (See Figure 5).

In total, 122 musically untrained subjects participated in the experiment. Importantly, the subjects were not familiar with the musical stimuli used in the study. Thus their associations were not determined by knowledge of the titles, lyrics, or self-reports of the composers.[173]

The main experiment consisted of a behavioral and a physiological part. In the behavioral part of the experiment, the subjects were asked to judge whether the

---

[171] *Ibid.*, p. 303.

[172] The table was acquired from http://www.stefan-koelsch.de/stimulus_repository.html.

[173] *Ibid.*, p. 306.

meaning of the prime stimulus is related to the meaning of the target word. Their judgments were collected separately for the linguistic and the musical primes.[174]

The physiological part of the experiment consisted in recording the neurological reactions of the subjects while they were being primed. A total of 176 significant prime-target pairs were selected for the EEG recording.[175]

Results

In the behavioral part of the experiment, the participants judged whether the prime and target stimuli were semantically related. The behavioral results show that the subjects' performance was high above chance for both musical and linguistic stimuli: they correctly categorized 80% of the target words after a musical excerpt, and 92% after sentences. 'Correctly' in this case means that the answers of the participants replicated the judgments on semantic (un)relatedness obtained in the pre-experiment.[176]

The physiological results, measured during the behavioral task, complement the behavioral results. They showed a larger N400 amplitude in cases where the participants were presented with semantically *unrelated* stimuli, compared to when they were presented with semantically *related* ones, and this is consistent with the results of previous research on the behavior of N400 in semantic priming experiments.

This gives evidence of the classical semantic priming effect that is already known to exist for the linguistic case, but was never tested for the relationship between instrumental music and words. The physiological aspect of the semantic priming effect did not differ between the language domain and the music domain with respect to latency, amplitude or scalp distribution. These findings suggest that music

---

[174] *Ibid.*, p. 306.

[175] *Ibid.*, p. 306.

[176] Koelsch et al., "Music, Language and Meaning," pp. 303-4.

can convey considerably more semantic information than assumed so far.[177] The examples of both types of primes and the changes in the N400 amplitude are shown in Figure 5.

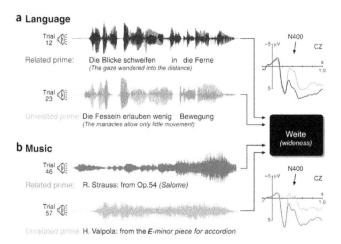

Figure 5: Examples of linguistic and musical primes. The primes semantically related to the word 'wideness' evoke a higher N400 amplitude, as seen on the right side of the image.[178]

Additional Experiments: Replicating the Results

The results obtained in the main experiment were fairly surprising – it did not seem to make a difference whether words were primed with sentences or with musical excerpts. The performance success in semantically priming words with music was almost as high as for the sentence-primes. The physiological reactions after musical and linguistic primes were even more similar.

In order to test the robustness of these results, two additional studies were conducted. They were designed as variations of the main experiment. In the first variation, only the physiological reactions were measured. The participants were not

---

[177] *Ibid.*, p. 304.

[178] Image was acquired from Koelsch et al., "Music, Language and Meaning," p. 303.

informed about the semantic relationships between primes and targets, but were instead told they were doing a memory test, while the neurological reactions were measured in the same way as in the main experiment. This variation tested whether the same physiological indicator of the semantic priming effect occurs when the participants do not pay attention to the semantic relatedness between the stimuli.[179]

In the second variation, the participants were presented with the same primes as in the main experiment, but instead of one target word, the primes were followed by a visually presented five-word list. The list involved two words already used in the main experiment for those primes (as a related and an unrelated target word), along with three other words randomly chosen from the pool of target words of the main experiment. The participants were asked to select one word from the five-word list that had the best semantic fit to the prime stimulus.[180]

The results of both experimental variations replicated the data of both pre-experiment and the main experiment. In the first variation, semantically unrelated target words elicited a visible rise of the N400 amplitude after both linguistic and musical primes. The amplitude of the N400 was practically identical as in the main experiment, replicating the physiological effects of the main experiment, and indicating that the physiological aspect of the semantic priming effect does not depend on the conscious judgements of the subjects regarding the semantic relations.[181]

In the second variation, after the linguistic primes, the participants selected the correct target word out of the five-word list in 86% of the trials, performing significantly above chance (chance was set at 20%). After musical primes, they selected the correct word in 58% of trials, which is also significantly above the 20% chance level.[182]

---

[179] *Ibid.*, p. 305.

[180] *Ibid.* Again, none of the subjects participated in any of the other versions of the experiment.

[181] *Ibid.*, p. 305.

[182] *Ibid.*

These results jointly support the conclusion that music can, just as language, prime the meaning of a word, and also demonstrate physiological indicators of semantic processing.

Control experiment for the emotional content

It may be objected that the target words used in the experiment possess emotional content, and that this emotional content may have interfered with the semantic priming effect, especially with the musical primes. It seems possible that musical excerpts might have primed words according to the emotional content they share with the target words. A control experiment was additionally conducted to test this possibility. A separate group of 26 participants was asked to rate the emotional content of each target word, on a scale ranging from 'strong negative content' to 'strong positive content', with 'emotionally neutral content' in the middle. This control study was designed to test whether the target words perhaps differ significantly in their emotional content, which would lead to the interference of the emotional and the conceptual content. If the two target words that are presented after the same prime (the semantically related, and the semantically unrelated target) did not differ significantly in their emotional content ratings, they were categorized as 'emotionally balanced'. The ratings showed that for 64% of the primes, the two target words matched with the prime were emotionally balanced.[183]

When the physiological effects were calculated separately for the emotionally balanced and unbalanced pairs of targets, the results showed no difference between these two groups in the N400 amplitude. This suggests that the emotional content of target words did not interfere with the physiological aspect of the semantic priming effect, and that the musical stimuli did not merely prime the participants' emotional states of which matched or failed to match the emotional content of target words.[184]

---

[183] *Ibid.*, p. 306.

[184] Koelsch et al., *op. cit.*, 304-5.

Implications of the Results

This study consisted of five experiments: the pre-experiment, the main experiment, the two variations, and the emotional content control experiment. Each experiment was performed with a different group of participants. When combined, the results of all five experiments jointly show, first, that musically untrained subjects who are presented with unfamiliar musical passages form similar associations between the passages and particular words. This suggests that the subjects found similar semantic content in the musical excerpts. Second, the corresponding neurological results indicate that the semantic priming effect occurs in the musical as well as in the language domain. The *auditory* perception of musical and linguistic primes similarly affected the participants' semantic processing when subsequently they were *visually* presented with the target words. This can be taken to suggest that music can influence processing of words just as language can. This further indicates that music can transfer semantically meaningful information and prime representations of concepts, independently of their emotional content.

Thus, it seems that meaning in music can include at least some conceptual content, embedded within the musical form itself, without extra-musical signs, and this conceptual content need not be emotion laden at all.

This implication is philosophically interesting due to the fact that it challenges both main philosophical positions concerning musical meaning – the formalists and expressionists. The two opposing positions both reject the possibility of music conveying conceptual content (especially abstract content), and instead argue whether music can convey emotional meaning without conceptual content (see Section 1.1), or whether it cannot convey definite emotional meaning at all (see Section 1.2). The conclusions of the presented study demonstrate that the only point of agreement between the debating philosophical parties is doubtful at least. Even Meyer's more permissive pluralistic view does not consider the possibility of conceptual meaning in music. His terminology allows it to be coined as extra-musical intellectual meaning, but it is unclear whether Meyer himself would allow it.

Conclusion of the First Chapter

This chapter presented three philosophical views on the meaning that can arise from music. In summary, the expressionists advocate for the emotional meaning in music which arises out of presenting, imitating, expressing, evoking or in other ways associating the listeners with particular emotions, most often by referring to emotions through the use of the already existing correspondences between musical elements and aspects of particular emotions. The formalists, on the other hand, defend the primacy of the specifically musical kind of meaning which consists in musical ideas or tone-ideas manifested in the musical structure itself. Finally, Meyer's pluralistic view differentiates between different aspects of meaning in music, making a distinction between intramusical (non-designative) and extra-musical (designative) *source* of meaning. Non-designative meaning arises out of the interplay of the listeners' musical expectations (expectations about the relationships between musical elements and about the course of events in music), while the designative meaning depends on the relationships established between music and the extra-musical events and phenomena (through association, reference, etc.). Meyer also distinguishes between emotional and intellectual *kind* of meaning. Meyer's account allows different combinations of these aspects. The kinds of meaning postulated by the expressionists and the formalists are renamed in Meyer's terms into extra-musical emotional meaning, and intramusical intellectual meaning, respectively. In other words, expressionist meaning is emotional meaning which depends on the relationships between music and extra-musical world, while the formalistic meaning consists in intellectually grasping the tonal relationships in the music itself. Another possible kind of meaning added by Meyer is the so-called intramusical emotional meaning – the emotional meaning established purely through the tension-resolution patterns in musical structure, without extra-musically referring to particular emotions.

Prima facie it was not clear how these views might be connected to the neurological and behavioral experiments on the reactions to music. However, the results of some such experiments provided interesting insights for the philosophical debates.

Relevance of the First Experiment

The first experiment showed that listeners with no musical training perceive meaning in musical structure alone, even without help of any extra-musical signs. This conclusion is based on the result that certain structural modifications in musical stimuli (as short as five-chord sequences) evoked in the participants neurological reactions characteristic for detecting semantic changes, similar to the reactions to semantic changes in language.

This conclusion is in accord with the formalistic idea of the existence of specifically musical meaning which consists in musical ideas, and lies in the formal relationships of music. If modifications of the formal structure also alter the idea (i.e., the meaning) of a musical sequence, this should be reflected in the listeners' neurological reactions characteristic for semantic processing, and this is exactly what was observed in the experiment.

The conclusion seems also to fit Meyer's view that listeners can find non-designative meaning in music through fulfillment or violation of their musical expectations, where the expectations are acquired simply by frequent exposure to music, without musical training. The modifications made to the short sequences consisted only in a violation of harmonic relationships expected in Western music (the tradition which the participants are familiar with). This violation of expectations concerning the ending of the musical sequence was reflected in the participants' neurological reactions. More precisely, the violation of expectations in music correlated with a change in neurological activity characteristic for processing the semantically unexpected input. This correlation suggests a connection between musical expectations and the processing of meaning in music.

In addition, establishing the existence of the semantic level in musical structure alone opens the space of possibilities for interpreting what musical semantics might be. One possibility was suggested in the Discussion of the first experiment (see Section 2.1 for more detail): musical syntax can be understood as the group of rules defining certain musical style or genre. Musical semantics, or the meaning of the musical structure consists in 'tone-ideas' that the composer wished to express within a given style or genre (i.e., compliant with the syntax of the style).

Methodological Insights

Apart from supporting the philosophical accounts of meaning in music, this experiment additionally provides a methodological insight into how the methods and facts of one discipline (such as neurocognitive science) can be relevant for a seemingly disparate discipline (such as musical aesthetics).

The problem of meaning concerns the level of phenomena: it concerns music or language themselves. It is difficult to find all answers about meaning by exploring it solely on the level of the phenomena, as we have seen from the ever unresolved philosophical debates. The ingenuity of this experiment is in transposing the problems of syntax and semantics in music and language onto the neurological level, where several novel, previously unavailable facts helped in testing hypotheses about meaning. The method of this experimental study consisted of several mutually related elements:

First, the already postulated *syntactic* analogy between music and language: they both possess rules and regularities regarding their structural organization according to which their instances (musical sequences or linguistic utterances) are constructed. When these rules are broken, anyone familiar with certain musical style or certain language is able to recognize the violation;

Second, the fact that language possesses a syntactic and a semantic level;

Third, the previously acquired result that there are neurological reactions related to changes in syntax and semantics of the linguistic input;

Fourth, the result that harmonic irregularity in the musical input also evokes characteristic neurological reactions;

Fifth, the *physiological* similarity (in amplitude of the brainwave) between the characteristic reaction to harmonic irregularities (N500) and the reaction to semantically unexpected sentences (N400).

Sixth, the previously acquired result that music and language share processing resources dedicated to structural integration of auditory input – interpreted as sharing resources for syntactic processing.

Finally, the result that the mentioned processing resources are limited.

Along with combining all of these previously acquired results and facts, the experimenters recorded behavioral and neurological reactions of the participants

66

simultaneously with the presentation of the musical and linguistic input, and measured possible interference between their reactions while comparing the changes made to the input. The novel results combined with the previously gathered ones provided sufficient evidence that on the neurological level it is plausible to posit a semantic analogy between music and language (in addition to the syntactic one).

In short, by combining a number of experimental results and certain linguistic facts (and also the knowledge of the style of Western music), the experimenters demonstrated the plausibility of postulating a semantic analogy between music and language on the neurological level. Postulating the semantic analogy on the neurological level provided support to a conception of musical syntax and semantics which are both embedded in the musical structure. It is hard to imagine how the conclusions about meaning on the level of phenomena (music and language) could have been reached from the armchair philosophical approach alone.

Relevance of the Second Experiment

The second experiment demonstrated a direct link between musical expectations and the emotions felt by the listeners in response to music. It also showed that structural changes in music alone can create tension and suspense in the listeners according to the principles of harmonic distance. The results of this experiment suggest that structural features of music, and expectation concerning these features may be important for the emotional meaning found in music.

The correlations between musical expectation and the emotional reactions found in this experiment fit with Meyer's conception of intramusical emotional meaning which is elicited through the interplay of musical expectations. This support is, however, limited. The structural changes in music (more precisely, the unexpectedness of the musical sequences) correlated only with the degree of *intensity* of the emotional response, and did not relate to any other aspects of emotion, or indicate how the musical structure might be differently related to different emotions.

This limitation might, however, be beneficial for the expressionist account of emotional meaning in music. The expressionists might claim that the correspondences that they posit between musical elements and particular emotions are necessary for the structural features of music to evoke different emotions. In other words, the tension-resolution patterns might only account for the general arousal of the listener, while the correspondences could be what turns this general arousal into a more specific emotional experience.

Methodological Insights

This experiment also relied on methods and facts unavailable from the armchair philosophical perspective. It is methodologically interesting because it combined musicological knowledge (of the principles of harmonic distance) and the previous results on the physiology of emotions. It also used self-reports and introspection of the participants, characteristic for experimental psychological research, but in combination with musical stimuli with differing properties.

The crucial technique used in the experiment was constructing a *range* of harmonic unexpectedness, instead of merely operating with a binary expected/unexpected groups of stimuli. The physiological reactions, as well as the ratings of the emotional impact can also be gradually measured. Thus, gradualness in the stimuli enabled gaining a richer picture concerning the correlations between the properties of musical stimuli and the emotional reactions. Since the physiological and subjective measures showed gradual increase proportional to the increase in harmonic unexpectedness, this provided assurance concerning the robustness of the correlations.

The neurological indicators of processing unexpectedness in the musical input (known from the previous research) were also used to support the connection between the musically unexpected events and the emotional reactions, since these indicators showed that the irregularity was registered by the listeners, even if only unconsciously.

Finally, the ability to construct a range of harmonic unexpectedness depended on knowing the principles of harmonic distance. In order to construct an experiment such as this, a certain degree of knowledge of music theory is necessary, along with the knowledge of the physiology of emotions. Thus, neither experimental psychologists nor musicologists alone could have reached the conclusions gained by this experiment. It is important to notice that these interdisciplinarily reached conclusions are relevant for testing the abstract philosophical hypotheses concerning the emotional meaning in music.

Relevance of the Third Experiment

The third experiment showed that the classical semantic priming experiment can be applied to test the semantic relations between music and language. More importantly, it showed that instrumental musical sequences are able to prime words in the same way as linguistic sentences.

The results of this experiment provided several insights interesting for the philosophical debates on meaning in music. First, they showed that even listeners without musical training are able to perceive *conceptual* content in at least some music, and, second, that they similarly perceive *what* that conceptual content is. The third insight is provided by the neurological results of the experiments, which confirm the existence of the semantic priming effect between music and concepts even on the neurological level.

This experiment provides maybe the most interesting insights for the philosophical debates, since it demonstrates the possibility of conveying conceptual meaning through musical structure alone. The results imply the possibility of, to use Meyer's terminology, 'intramusical conceptual meaning': conceptual meaning which is achieved by purely musical resources, something that was not mentioned in any of the philosophical discussions of musical meaning, or, if mentioned, was dismissed out of hand.

The implications of this experiment also show that empirical research can be used not only to decide between competing philosophical positions, but also to suggest new possibilities for the philosophical analysis.

Methodological Insights

The unexpected results of the third experiment were achieved by only slightly changing a classical experiment already widely in use in experimental psychology. The experimenters hypothesized the existence of a semantic analogy between music and language, and tested the interaction between their semantic contents, both behaviorally and neurologically. The methodological innovation consisted in altering the semantic priming experiment so that it involves stimuli from both musical and linguistic domain. The relationships between such mixed stimuli were tested by using musical sequences as primes for the target words, and then comparing whether there are similarities and differences in the priming effect when the stimuli are taken from only one (linguistic) domain, and when the stimuli are mixed (i.e., musical sequences and words).

The procedure of this experiment also relied on the extensive knowledge of music theory and history. Musical stimuli were chosen based on several factors, some of which involved knowledge of musicological terminology (e.g., 'wide/narrow positions of intervals'), or self-reports of the composers (such as Schoenberg describing parts of his compositions as related to his heart surgery). Again, a fair degree of interdisciplinarity was necessary in order to construct this kind of experiment and choose the musical sequences which could bring about interesting results.

***

These experiments jointly show that interdisciplinary research is relevant for the philosophical debates on musical meaning, because it introduces numerous arguments which would otherwise not be available to the philosophers, since they rely on facts and methods not commonly used in armchair philosophy.

Apart from this methodological point, these experiments show that musical meaning can be of various kinds. Along with the specifically musical meaning implied by the first experiment, the results of the second and the third experiment imply that the tonal structures alone can convey extra-musical meanings. This directly supports Meyer's claims about intramusical emotional meaning (see Section 1.3). It also fits with Robinson's claim that there might be several mutually incompatible interpretations of the same musical material (see Section 1.1). Each interpretation might focus on one kind of meaning arising from music, and also to the combinations and interactions between these meanings. Further analysis can lead us to the idea that these kinds of meaning do not exclude each other: music may well be apt for exhibiting simultaneously several levels of meaning solely by its structure, and these kinds of meaning possibly (or rather probably) interact and interfere with each other.

Chapter 2 – Value of Music

In the previous chapter, it was already mentioned that one of the key components of the appraisal of a musical work is judging its value. Judging the value of a work is tightly related to the existence of criteria according to which the judgment is made. In regard to the possibility of existence of such criteria, two main views are at the forefront of the philosophical aesthetics: first, the objectivist view which advocates attributing objectivity to musical value and to the criteria of judgment, and, second, the subjectivist view which denies any such objectivity and maintains that the criteria are relative to the subject's point of view. In addition to these two positions, there is also a more complex and interesting view on musical value: the dispositionalist view which attempts to reconcile objectivist and subjectivist intuitions by an explanation of the relationship between the aesthetic object and the perceiving subject.

After presenting the key claims of the former two views, I will dedicate most of the philosophical part of the chapter to a modified version of Hume's dispositionalist account. Even though Hume did not originally focus on music, I believe that his account, when adapted to music, can enable us to forge a connection between the supposedly objective aesthetic criteria debated by philosophers and the conclusions of contemporary experimental psychology of music. Hume's emphasis on the empirical means for determining specific answers with regard to aesthetic value is, I believe, what makes this connection at least conceptually possible.[185]

The goal of this chapter will be to show how the assumptions of the dispositionalist approach in aesthetics can facilitate establishing connections between the results of the empirical research and one of the most abstract concepts of philosophical aesthetics – the concept of value in music. The middle part of the chapter will focus on the experimental research related to musical preferences and sensitivity to musical features – the empirical counterparts of the aesthetic concepts of

---

[185] David Hume, "Of the Standard of taste," in *Essays Moral, Political, and Literary*, ed. T. H. Green and T. H. Grose (London, 1882), p. 279.

value and expertise, respectively. The aim of the chapter will be to demonstrate and establish the relevance of the experimental methods and results presented for the debates among the aestheticians.

1 Philosophical Theories of Musical Value

1.1 Objectivism and Subjectivism of Aesthetic Value

Throughout the history of aesthetics, the problem of aesthetic value was generally seen in terms of the controversy between two extreme positions. The objectivist view maintains that aesthetic value is an inherent property of objects, whether belonging to the order of nature or the realm of art. The value of the object is determined by its properties and is independent of the subject's reactions to it. Consequently, not all judgments concerning aesthetic value are equally justified. Some of them (the ones that coincide with the objective fact concerning the value of the object) are correct, while others are false. The objectivity of aesthetic judgments is thus tightly related to the status of aesthetic value as a property of the aesthetic object.[186]

The opposing view denies that aesthetic value is an inherent property of objects themselves and maintains that it is human subjects who assign such value to objects, on the basis of their own responses and preferences. But none of these subjective responses to, and preferences regarding, a given object, e.g. a musical work, are in principle better founded or more justified than any other, and thus the view is not merely subjectivist but also relativist. The object's formal and other non-aesthetic properties are merely what occasions the subjects' response. Since judgments concerning the aesthetic value do not refer to any objective property, it seems inevitable that all are on a par, none more justified than any others. They are all merely expressions of personal tastes and preferences, similar to the judgments concerning what is pleasant, attractive, etc. Aesthetic subjectivism comes in various degrees of sophistication.[187], but all forms of it share the basic denial of objectivity and find it very difficult to avoid commitment to relativism.

---

[186] Leon Kojen, "Hume On the Standard of Taste" ["Hjum o merilu ukusa"], in *Art and Value* [*Umetnost i vrednost*] (Beograd: Filip Višnjić, 1989), pp. 156-7.

[187] Wladyslaw Tatarkiewicz, "Objectivity and Subjectivity in the History of Aesthetics," *Philosophy and Phenomenological Research* 24, no. 2 (1963): p. 157.

Both of these extreme views have their own specific drawbacks. The objectivist definition of value ignores the relevance of the subject's experience to aesthetic judgment, while the subjectivist view leaves out the properties of the object judged: both of these components, at least intuitively, seem too important to the concept of aesthetic value to be left out. Apart from these extreme views, there is a 'middle' position that seems to accommodate crucial parts of the two opposed views in a fairly satisfying way. This is the dispositionalist view, most articulately developed by Hume:[188] Hume introduces it as an account of the concept of beauty, but it can be adapted to the concept of aesthetic value, which is the focus of this chapter.[189]

---

[188] Even though Hume's aesthetic theory is often mistakenly interpreted as radically subjectivist, a careful reading reveals him to be a dispositionalist about beauty. Here I will follow an interpretation based on a systematic reconstruction of his argumentation given by Leon Kojen in *Art and Value*. I choose this interpretation because, apart from being more faithful to Hume's original intentions and better supported by his text, it renders his view more coherent and tenable (and thus more interesting) than the other interpretations.

[189] Even though many authors relevant to musical aesthetics consider them as equivalent (most explicitly Hanslick, *On the Musically Beautiful*), I will take beauty and aesthetic value as different concepts, and in this chapter I will focus on the concept of aesthetic value. In order to make the conceptual relations clear, I will adopt Beardsley's view of the relationship between beauty and value in stating that beauty is a sufficient but not a necessary condition of aesthetic value. This is to say, first, that "A fairly high degree of beauty is a sufficient condition of a fairly high degree of aesthetic value." [Monroe C. Beardsley, "Beauty and Aesthetic Value," *Journal of Philosophy* 59, no. 21 (1962): p. 626.] Beardsley explains this by saying that anyone who can say that this is a beautiful piece of music can also say that it is a good piece of music. He justifies this by further stating that the conditions of being a good piece of music are multiple. But if beauty in a piece of music is sufficient to make it good, that must be because beauty has itself complex conditions that are also conditions of musical value. Second, beauty is not a necessary condition of aesthetic value. It is only one ground of aesthetic value. Beardsley illustrates this with a musical example: "(…) I would say, for example, that Beethoven's Great Fugue (Op. 133) should not be called beautiful, though it is a tremendous piece of music, a great and excellent work. Parts of it have beauty, but as a whole it glories in its power, its dramatic intensity, its drive and pent-up energy." [Beardsley, *op.cit.*, 626-7.]

1.2 The Dispositionalist Account

The fundamental claim of Hume's dispositional account of beauty is that "beauty is such an order and construction of parts, as either by the primary constitution of our nature, by custom, or by caprice, is fitted to give a pleasure and satisfaction to the soul."[190] In other words, certain *objective* features (an order and construction of parts) of an artwork are suitable to evoke a specific *subjective* response (pleasure and satisfaction), owing to either something permanent and universal (human nature), or to something non-universal but widely shared and of fairly long duration (custom in the sense of traditions specific to a given culture), or finally owing to something purely individual and thus idiosyncratic (caprice). Hume's definition thus incorporates the relevant properties of the aesthetic object as well as the responses of the perceiving subjects, and also, as the third component, the various factors one of which is necessary if the given objective features are to produce the relevant specific response.[191]

Since it is musical value that is the subject matter of this chapter, the relevant formulation of dispositionalism will be as follows: the musical value is determined by certain (objective) properties of the musical work,[192] but it is also suitable to prompt the perceiving subjects to a specific type of response – such as showing preference toward the musical piece and assigning value to it, given that the subject satisfies the appropriate long-term and short-term conditions. Thus, even though musical value is constituted by the properties of the object (musical work), it is only possible to have knowledge of it because it is being recognized, and consequently preferred by the appropriate perceiving subjects. This definition might seem quite vague and even circular, but all of its components will be clarified in the following discussion.

---

[190] David Hume, *Treatise of Human Nature*, reprinted from the Original Edition in three volumes and edited by L.A. Selby-Bigge, M.A. (Oxford: Clarendon Press, 1896), Bk II, Pt 1, Section 8: Of Beauty and Deformity, pp. 299-300.

[191] Kojen, *op. cit.*, pp. 133-7.

[192] These properties can also be relational properties, in order to take account of the cultural context of the musical piece.

The relationship between value, on the one hand, and the subjects' preferences and appreciation on the other can be understood similarly to the relationship which Kant posits between freedom of will and the moral law: the relationship between the *ratio essendi* and the *ratio cognoscendi*.[193] I will briefly elaborate on how I conceive this relationship.

Namely, it is a fact that there exists, in different cultures and different epochs, a systematic practice of engaging in activities which include praising, assigning value, or showing appreciation toward certain kinds of artefacts or artworks. These activities can be understood as varieties of aesthetic appreciation, and can, of course, be manifested in different ways, directed at different objects, and motivated by different criteria. It can be argued, however, that, throughout history, there subsists the idea that certain artefacts or works of art are highly valuable – musical works among other things – even though there might not be an agreement concerning which works and why.[194] I believe that this idea is a constitutive element of the activity of aesthetic appreciation.

---

[193] Immanuel Kant, *Critique of Practical Reason*, ed. Mary J. Gregor (Cambridge: Cambridge University Press, 1788/1997), p. 5:5n. Apart from Kant, I also draw inspiration from the already mentioned interpretation of Hume's definition of the standard of taste, in Kojen, "Hume On the Standard of Taste" ["Hjum o merilu ukusa"], 193-6. According to Kojen, Hume defines the standard of taste – the criterion by which beauty is to be judged – as both "the rules of beauty" and "the joint verdict of the 'good critics'". Kojen construes the relationship between the two *definientia* and the *definiendum* as a relationship between the *ratio essendi* and the *ratio cognoscendi*, respectively. He takes the rules of beauty to be the *ratio essendi* of the standard of taste, in the sense that these rules are what determines which aesthetic judgments are justified and which are not. The "joint verdict of the good critics" he takes to be the *ratio cognoscendi* of the standard of taste, in the sense that the judgement of those individuals who are in an epistemically privileged position (what this is will be elaborated in the following section) is what guides us toward the standard of taste – their "joint verdict" reveals which of the aesthetic judgments are in accord with the rules of beauty and which are not.

[194] Hume goes even further to claim that there are works that are universally appreciated: "The same Homer, who pleased at Athens and Rome two thousand years ago, is still admired at Paris and at London." – Hume, "Of the Standard of Taste," p. 271. I believe that accepting

I take this fact – the systematic practice of aesthetic appreciation – to be the *ratio cognoscendi* of aesthetic value. Applied to music, it means that we only learn of musical value through the awareness of the special status and systematic appreciation of certain musical works, even though in practice people may not agree which musical works exactly have this special status.

Furthermore, the musical value, constituted by the works' properties, can be understood as the *ratio essendi*, "the reason of the existence", of the kind of systematic appreciation and preference it evokes in the perceiving subjects. This is not an assumption that can be demonstrated or refuted. I only wish to posit this kind of mutually constitutive relationship as a possibility, in order to open the way for connecting the abstract and normative concept of value with empirical facts, and open up the issue of aesthetic value (i.e., make it accessible) to empirical research. Although value itself is difficult (or impossible) to investigate empirically, the subjective responses related to it, such as preferences – an empirical indicator correlated with the degree of value the subject assigns to the work of art – are already being researched in many areas of empirical investigation, such as psychology, neurology, etc.

Accepting the assumption of 'Kantian' relationship between objective value and subjective responses would make empirical research more interesting for the philosophy of music, and *vice versa*. It still needs to be shown in detail how the criteria for making justified aesthetic judgments fit this general idea. Namely, dispositionalism, just like objectivism, takes some judgments of aesthetic value to be more justified than others. Here I will once again rely on Hume's account (in Kojen's interpretation) and adopt the view that the joint verdict of individuals who stand in an epistemically privileged position (to be explained below) provides the criteria for the justification of the subjective judgments.[195] More importantly, by emphasizing the importance of the differences between the perceiving subjects for determining these

---

even a weaker claim of universally having *some* works as highly appreciated is sufficient for establishing the metaphysical possibility I am interested in, as I will elaborate in the rest of the chapter.

[195] See Hume, "Of the Standard of Taste," pp. 278-9., and also Kojen, *op. cit.*, pp. 193-6.

criteria, dispositionalism makes it possible to connect experimental psychological research with the aesthetic problem of musical value. The next section will show the philosophical relevance of the perceiving subjects reacting differently to musical works.

Differences Between the Perceiving Subjects

One important advantage of the dispositionalist view is that it accommodates two seemingly contradictory facts. First, it acknowledges the fact that there is a variety of taste and preference concerning musical works – Hume himself opens his essay with the observation that this variety is obvious to everyone, and that it prompts many people to hold the subjectivist view concerning the aesthetic value. Nevertheless dispositionalism also acknowledges the fact that, despite the obvious variety in taste and preference, there is an indisputable general intuition that some aesthetic judgments are considered by almost everyone to be obviously false, or at least less justified than their contraries, for example, the judgment that 'any composition of Frantisek Kotzwara is equally, or more aesthetically valuable than any of the Beethoven's symphonies'.[196]

The dispositionalist theory deals with these two facts by insisting on the difference between the perceiving subjects, and claiming that because of this not all aesthetic judgments are equally justified: even though any perceiving subject may pronounce on the value of musical works, only few are qualified to make a proper judgment, or establish their own preferences as the criterion of value.[197] There are two groups of qualities that make the subjects 'stand in an epistemically privileged position', as mentioned earlier in the chapter. First, in order to count as a 'true judge', to use Hume's term, the subject must have the appropriate long-term capabilities

---

[196] Hume's example of a clearly false aesthetic judgement would be to "assert an equality of genius and elegance between Ogilby and Milton." According to Hume, "the principle of the natural equality of tastes is then totally forgot", "(…) and we pronounce without scruple the sentiment of these pretended critics to be absurd and ridiculous." – Hume, "Of the Standard of Taste," p. 269.

[197] *Ibid.*, 278-9.

which have to do with culture, experience, a high degree of refinement, etc. Second, the subject must actually be in an appropriate state: properly attentive to the work, perceptually and emotionally undisturbed, etc., since "in each creature, there is a sound and a defective state, and the former alone can be supposed to afford us a true standard of taste (…)", but also be already acquainted with the work of art in question.[198] Hume appeals to an analogy with visual perception, especially perception of color (understood as a Lockean secondary quality), in order to point out that the objectivity of aesthetic judgments is not an isolated phenomenon:[199] "in like manner as the appearance of objects in daylight, to the eye of a man in health, is denominated their true and real colour, even while colour is allowed to be merely a phantasm of the senses."[200] Thus, even though aesthetic judgments are subjective in a sense that they depend on the state of the subject, they are also capable of being objectively justified, depending on whether the subject is in an epistemically privileged position.

When speaking about epistemically privileged subjects, it is natural to consider the possibility of such subjects disagreeing in aesthetic judgments. Hume's view allows for such disagreements. He claims that there are differences in aesthetic judgment which do not result from differences in capacities (in 'delicacy of taste'), but can instead be attributed to differences of either individual inclinations: "the different humours of particular men," or of the external factors such as "the particular manners and opinions of our age and country."[201] We can understand this as meaning that the 'true judge' is someone who has developed the capacities for recognizing all the aesthetically relevant features of musical works. This, however, does not entail that the true judge is deprived of preferences within the 'good taste'. To take the example of wine experts, which Hume also mentions,[202] while two experts may both detect the slightest details in the taste of wine, one may prefer sweet to sour wine, while the other may prefer the opposite. In regard to such diversity of taste which is a

---

[198] *Ibid.*, 271-2, 274-9.

[199] Kojen, *op. cit.*, p. 169.

[200] Hume, *op. cit.*, 272.

[201] *Ibid.*, 280-1.

[202] *Ibid.*, 272-3.

result of the factors accidental and not aesthetically relevant, Hume replies that "in that case a certain degree of diversity in judgment is unavoidable, and we seek in vain for a standard, by which we can reconcile the contrary sentiments."[203] In application to music, in case of disagreements concerning, for example, whether Bach's works are better than Mozart's, the delicacy of taste enables the disagreeing parties to agree on what they observe in the musical works, and on their aesthetically relevant features, but it does not entail overcoming personal inclinations.[204] Therefore the existence of disagreement among the experts does not by itself oppose the objectivity of their judgments. The factors that they disagree on may, in other words, be aesthetically irrelevant.

Hume admits that the persons that fulfill all the prerequisites will certainly be rare, and whether any particular person is endowed with all those qualities may "be the subject of dispute, and be liable to discussion and enquiry."[205] This, however, is not a theoretical problem for the dispositionalist view – who are 'the experts' in some specific art, or genre, may be regarded as an empirical question. For Hume, it is sufficient that we accept "that the taste of all individuals is not upon an equal footing,"[206] however hard it may be to determine empirically which individuals are in fact endowed with all the requisite qualities.[207] Applying this to the topic of this chapter – *if* it can be demonstrated that someone is an expert for making aesthetic judgments with regard to certain art forms, their judgments should be able to direct us toward the criteria of musical value. For if who the experts are can be determined empirically, then we can approach value in music (through the experts' judgments) empirically as well. Once again, accepting the possibility of objective criteria for

---

[203] *Ibid.*, 280-1.

[204] Hume himself gives the following example: "A young man, whose passions are warm, will be more sensibly touched with amorous and tender images, than a man more advanced in years, who take pleasure in wise, philosophical reflections concerning the conduct of life and moderation of the passions. At twenty, Ovid may be the favourite author; Horace at forty; and perhaps Tacitus at fifty." – see Hume, *op. cit.*, 281.

[205] *Ibid.*

[206] *Ibid.*

[207] *Ibid.*, 271-9.

aesthetic judgments forges a connection between the empirical research and the abstract philosophical and aesthetic problems.

It should be noted that, even though we have adopted Hume's general argumentation in developing the dispositionalist account of aesthetic value, we are not obliged to adopt his more specific arguments which appeal to the universality of human nature in establishing the possibility of objective criteria for aesthetic judgments. Thus, even though Hume's view involves general rules, or 'rules of art' which define what renders a work of art aesthetically valuable, his account can also be modified to dispense with such general rules. The criteria for aesthetic judgments can instead rely on paradigmatic examples of aesthetically valuable works of art, recognized by the experts in aesthetic judgment.

Hume lists a number of traits or qualities necessary for expertise in aesthetic judgment: delicacy of taste, practice in judging a particular art (or genre), experience in making comparisons between artworks, good sense, and freedom from prejudice, etc.[208] Hume's proposal is mostly reasonable, although we are not obliged to agree fully with his list of traits. In the experimental part of the chapter, I will show how some of the capacities which are at work in the appraisal of musical works, and which can in some ways be related to Hume's proposed qualities, were empirically tested.[209]

---

[208] For the precise way Hume conceives of the last two qualities, see Kojen 180-187.

[209] It should be noted that the kinds of capacities that will be the focus of the empirical research are characteristic for music appraisal, and thus, the research strategy presented in this chapter works well for music. It is not clear how the capacities required for qualified judgments in other arts (especially, say, literature) could be empirically investigated, and whether a similar strategy could be beneficial for empirically approaching the aesthetical problems regarding other arts.

2 Experiments Related to Musical Value

2.1 Conceptual Connections: Value, Expertise, Preferences, and Sensitivity

The modified dispositional account presented in the previous section establishes a connection between musical value and the preferences of the qualified subjects. The experimental part of this chapter will explore the aspect of this view that is accessible to the empirical research – the subjects: their aesthetic judgments, understood as preferences toward the musical pieces, and their qualifications for making good aesthetic judgments.

The experimental part will thus have two focal points: musical preferences, and musical expertise. We will see that the research on preferences conducted so far does not provide the results sufficient for any interesting conclusions related to musical value, but can only be useful for exploring the short-term conditions for making adequate judgments, such as the ones mentioned in the dispositionalist account (see Section 1.2). Nevertheless, I will supplement the results from these studies with a few suggestions for some future research that might be more beneficial for the kind of aesthetic analysis that is the interest of this chapter. In regard to expertise, however, numerous studies are available which test the sensitivity of various kinds of subjects (experts and laypersons, infants, children and adults, and even animals) to different types of musical stimuli, and they do provide results with interesting implications. I propose that the way to empirically approach the concept of musical value is through two mutually related steps: by examining the musical preferences of various kinds of subjects, and by examining the differences in sensitivity of the same kinds of subjects.

It is also worth noting that, by exploring the reactions of the subjects, we will not stay limited to the subjective reports (and therefore the subjective aspect of musical value). Measuring their success in behavioral tasks, as well as the accompanying neurocognitive reactions will provide us with a certain degree of objectivity related to the subjective reactions. The experimental part of the chapter will, thus, try to find something objective on the subjective side of the dispositionalist dichotomy. All of this will be explained in detail in the following sections.

2.2 Empirical Research on Music Preference

When we engage in an analysis of the empirical research on music preferences, we can see that there is an abundance of studies researching the impact of a large number of different factors on music preferences. This might seem optimistic for the aims of this chapter: by knowing more about music preferences of various subjects, we might approach the problem of musical value with more information at hand. When we dig deeper, however, it becomes clear that the results of these studies are potentially misleading – that is, if we wish to infer from them conclusions regarding musical value. Namely, the preferences that are being researched in most of these studies are not the ones that are relevant for the aesthetic judgment, as well as the factors that influence these kinds of preferences. In the next section, I will demonstrate this through several points.

Theoretical Models of Music Preference

In his dissertation *Determinants of Music Preference*, Thomas Schaefer presents what is currently known about the factors that influence music preferences. Schaefer singles out four groups of factors which were found to have an influence on music preference. These factors concern: the music, the listener, the context, and the use of music.[210]

The first group involves the characteristics of the music. The studies report on the music preference being influenced by, for example, the level of loudness,[211]

---

[210] Thomas Schaefer, "Determinants of Music Preference" (PhD diss., Chemnitz University, 2008), pp. 6-10.

[211] Salvatore Cullari and Olga Semanchick, "Music Preferences and Perception of Loudness," *Perceptual and Motor Skills* 68, no. 1 (1989): 186.

tempo,[212] level of complexity,[213] familiarity,[214] or whether the listener is able to recognize the musical work as belonging to a particular style.[215] The second group includes the attributes of the listener, such as age, gender, socio-economic status, ethnic group, whether the listener is musically educated, etc. The third group of factors concerns the context of music listening: the cultural context, the social context, whether other people are present, etc. In order to illustrate this group of factors, Schaefer cites one study which showed that music preferences are highly dependent on the judgments of other people. The study found this dependence by experimenting with ratings of songs on an artificial market on the internet, where the participants did not know each other.[216] The fourth group of factors is related to the use of music – the function that the listener assigns to the music. People use music to fulfill various needs. Music can serve: emotional, cognitive, cultural, physiological and other functions. Some people use it to express their social identity, values or beliefs, to elicit or sustain pleasant emotions as well as to alleviate or change negative emotions, or to regulate the physiological arousal level.[217]

Even though there have been numerous studies exploring isolated factors in music preference, Schaefer notes that it is surprising that there were almost no attempts in the literature to offer a systematic theoretical account which would

---

[212] James J. Kellaris, "Consumer Aesthetics Outside the Lab: Preliminary Report on a Musical Field Study," *Advances in Consumer Research* 19 (1992): 730-734.

[213] See Daniel E. Berlyne, *Studies in the New Experimental Aesthetics: Steps Towards an Objective Psychology of Aesthetic Appreciation* (London: Halstead press, 1974). See also Ronald G. Heyduk, "Rated Preference for Musical Compositions as it Relates to Complexity and Exposure Frequency," *Perception and Psychophysics* 17, no. 1 (1975): 84-90.

[214] Adrian C. North and David J. Hargreaves, "Situational Influences on Reported Musical Preference," *Psychomusicology* 15, no. 1-2 (1996): 30-45.

[215] Colin Martindale and Kathleen Moore, "Relationship of Musical Preference to Collative, Ecological, and Psychophysical Variables," *Music Perception* 6, no. 4 (1989): 431-445.

[216] Matthew J. Salganik, Peter S. Dodds, and Duncan J. Watts, "Experimental Study of Inequality and Unpredictability in an Artificial Cultural Market," *Science* 311 (2006): 854-856.

[217] Schaefer, *op. cit.*, 6-10.

incorporate the results of these studies. He remarks that so far only two plausible theoretical accounts were offered. Both of them were integrating and systemizing the empirical results in a theoretical model, but only one of them was focused specifically on music preference.[218] The first model was developed by LeBlanc who suggested an "interactive theory of music preference". LeBlanc's model combines most of the factors that influence music preference discussed above and suggests that these factors interact on different levels in a hierarchical process. Schaefer praises LeBlanc's model for incorporating a great variety of factors, and also because it suggests that the interactions between these factors can be investigated empirically, although LeBlanc admits that the interactive nature of these factors makes each of them difficult to measure.[219]

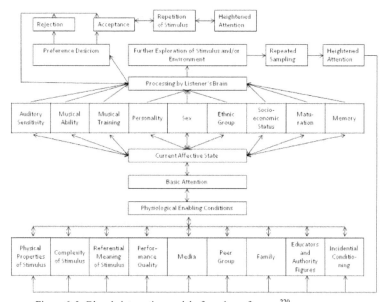

Figure 6: LeBlanc's interactive model of music preference.[220]

[218] Schaefer, *op. cit.*, p. 10.

[219] *Ibid*, p. 11.

[220] The image was acquired from Schaefer, "Determinants of Music Preference," p. 11.

The second suggested model – the so-called "reciprocal response model" adopts many factors from LeBlanc' model. This model is not focused specifically on music preference, but instead describes the factors which influence responses to music in general, and preferences are included as a part of the listener's general response.[221]

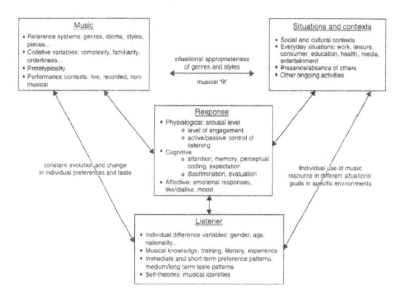

Figure 7: Hargreaves' reciprocal response model of music preference.[222]

This model describes how the three out of four groups of factors listed above (the music, the listener, and the listening context) interact with each other. The focus of the model is to describe "the determinants of an immediate response to a specific musical stimulus at a given point in time".[223]

It is not necessary to go into details of these theoretical models. It serves the purpose of this chapter to present them briefly as the most thorough and systematic work that was conducted on music preferences. Their relevance for the topic of this chapter, and the problem with relying on them as explanations of musical preferences

---

[221] *Ibid*, p. 13.

[222] The image was acquired from Schaefer, "Determinants of Music Preference," p. 13.

[223] *Ibid*.

in the debate on aesthetic judgments will be discussed below. Before that, it is helpful to show an example of one of the experimental studies that these theoretical models use as their basis.

Example of the Experimental Studies of Musical Preferences

As an example of how the experimental studies determine the relevance of a factor in influencing music preferences, I will shortly present Schaefer's own study that adds a factor not included in the existing systematic models. Schaefer was mostly interested in the possible correlation between the physiological changes which occur while listening to music, and the strength of music preference. More specifically, the aim of the study was testing whether physiological arousal enhances the 'liking' for a given piece of music. This hypothesis has not been examined before.[224] This study is especially interesting because it illustrates both the case when the external factor does influence the degree of music preference, and the case when there is no influence, as will be shown below.

The participants were thirty-six students with moderate experience with music. They were instructed to rate their preference for the musical pieces that were played to them – these were the subjective measures of the study. The study also recorded the physiological measures associated with changes in arousal, namely, heart rate, and skin conductance level.[225]

The stimuli consisted of six musical pieces, divided in two groups according to genre. The neutral or 'lounge' group consisted of three compositions in the 'lounge' genre ("Kleine Träumerei" by Moca, Blue Flame; "On the beach" by Rivera Rotation; "Dream" by Wei-Chi). The 'classical group' consisted of three compositions by Frederic Chopin ("Nocturnes Op. 15 No. 2 Fis-Dur"; "Impromptus

---

[224] Schaefer, *op. cit.*, p. 33.

[225] Schaefer, *op. cit.*, p. 26.

No. 2 Op. 36 Fis-Dur"; "Valses No. 13 Op. 70/3 Des-Dur"). The subjects have never heard any of the compositions included in the study.[226]

The method consisted in the following procedure. In both lounge condition and classical condition, the subjects listened to the three musical works within the given group. The arousal induction was implemented during either the second or the third composition, and the participants rated their preference for these pieces, while their physiological measures (mentioned above) were simultaneously recorded.[227]

The physiological arousal can be induced by several methods, and Schaefer opted for 'self-focused attention'. This technique consists in the subjects sitting in front of a mirror and observing and writing down how their facial expressions changed while listening to the music. The subjects were not informed about the purpose of the study, but were instead told that the study investigated musically induced changes in facial expression.[228]

If the arousal was successful, heart rate (HR), skin conductance (SC), and breathing rate (BR) should increase simultaneously with inducing arousal.[229] To analyze whether the arousal induction was successful, Schaefer calculated the measurements of arousal indicators over time in all three listenings. With the use of contrast analysis, Schaefer concluded that the time course of arousal induction corresponded to the predicted changes in these measures, suggesting that the arousal induction was successful.[230]

When the preference ratings were compared with the time course of the arousal induction, it was concluded that, for lounge music, in both arousal induction during the second and the third listening, there was a slight increase in the preference ratings which correlated with the arousal induction. Schaefer interpreted this part of

---

[226] *Ibid.*, p. 33.

[227] *Ibid.*, pp. 33-4.

[228] *Ibid.*

[229] *Ibid.*

[230] *Ibid.*, pp. 34-5.

the results as suggesting that the participants possibly perceived the increase in physiological arousal, and interpreted it as a positive emotional reaction to the music.[231]

The second part of the results, however, did not support the same hypothesis: for the classical compositions, there were no changes in preference ratings during arousal induction. It seems that even though the induction was successful, it had no influence on the preferences. Schaefer offered an explanation of this lack of influence. Namely, since classical music is more complex and contains more information than lounge music, listening to the classical compositions has perhaps required more attention from the subjects than lounge songs, and thus the subjects had insufficient resources to pay attention to their arousal.[232]

In summary, the results indicate that, in the lounge condition, the arousal induction correlated with higher preference, while in the classical condition there was no correlation.

Problems with Schaefer Type Studies

The conclusions of this study have a limited impact even for its own goal of investigation, due to the fact that the arousal effect did not occur in all conditions, but only for the neutral lounge music. Even though this fact could be used for inferring further interesting conclusions about the influence of arousal to different types of musical structures, they would not be relevant for the topic of this chapter. Namely, even though there is a rich body of empirical work on the multitude of factors which affect music preference, there are several problems with the use of separate findings (such as Schaefer's) and the theoretical models devised to systematize these findings (such as LeBlanc's and Hargreaves's models).

---

[231] *Ibid.*, pp. 36-7.

[232] *Ibid.*, pp. 34-7.

First, there are problems with the systemizing models on their own: the models are formulated in a rather vague fashion, and it is hard to derive concrete predictions about how single factors interact in the formation of music preference.[233] Second, even if the conclusions of the Schaefer study had more impact (e.g. if the results showed that the physiological arousal always significantly influences music preferences), and if the systemizing models were formulated in a more rigid way that would make them empirically verifiable, using them in the context of the aesthetic judgments would still be problematic. The conclusions of these studies do not address the preferences we are interested in when discussing the aesthetic judgments and musical value. The music preferences that they explain are understood in a sense that does not make them relatable to the aesthetic issues. Namely, these models only describe short-term preference decisions at one point in time. They can help to understand how someone decides for or against an actual piece of music, or they can be used to explore only the momentary states of the subject which Hume mentions (see Section 1.2), but they are not appropriate to explain the development of long-term preferences relevant for the aesthetic judgment that is the interest of this chapter. Also, they treat the listener as a passive agent who only responds to a given stimulus.[234]

Thus, if we only relied on experimental studies on preferences such as Schaefer's, or systematic theoretical models of preferences such as LeBlanc's or Hargreaves and colleagues', we could be mislead by the results: it might seem that there is far more interference of certain external factors, or irregularity in music preference than there actually is, because the preferences are understood in those accounts as short-term impressions or decisions at one point in time.

The relevance of presenting Schaefer's study in this chapter is in illustrating the method by which most studies on music preferences so far were conducted, and showing why we should be careful in taking over the conclusions about music preferences reached by experimental psychology, and implementing them in the context of philosophical aesthetics. What is of more interest for exploring the concept

---

[233] *Ibid.*, pp. 12-13.

[234] *Ibid.*, p. 14.

of value are instead long-term or permanent preferences, accumulated by a slow process of repeated listening mediated by the reasons applicable in making an aesthetic judgment.

Alternative Attempts at Testing of Music Preference

Some isolated studies do examine preferences over short and longer time-spans, their stability over time, and the factors that influence their development. Lamont and Webb for example, explored the factors that have an impact on both short- and long-term music preferences. However, the studies such as this also refer to the concept of preference that is not relevant for the analysis of the aesthetic judgment, because the sense of preference they explore is the *favorite* musical piece of a particular listener, either for a short or a long period.[235] Long-term favoring of a musical piece is indeed closer to the preference we are interested in than the momentary preferences examined in the Schaefer study. However, it still carries a connotation of *personal* taste, rather than a choice based on some (purportedly objective) aesthetic criteria.

The Aesthetically Relevant Sense of Preference

The sense of preference relevant for this chapter should carry the connotation of Kant's judgments of beauty, which, even though they are subjective judgments, make a claim to universal validity.[236] The preferences in this sense arise out of such aesthetic judgments which involve assigning aesthetic value to a musical piece based on the characteristically aesthetic reasons. The aesthetic reasons, unlike non-aesthetic reasons such as emotional significance, personal associations, popularity of the piece, etc., appeal to certain inherent or dispositional properties of the musical work.

---

[235] See Alexandra Lamont and Rebecca Webb, "Short- and Long-Term Musical Preferences: What Makes a Favourite Piece of Music?" *Psychology of Music* 38, no. 2 (2010): 222-241.

[236] Immanuel Kant, *Critique of the Power of Judgment*, trans. Paul Guyer and Eric Matthews, (Cambridge: Cambridge University Press, 2000), Second Moment, §6-9, 5:211–219, pp. 96-104.

Although it is hard to precisely determine the properties which the aesthetic reasons appeal to, it is possible to cite enough examples of such properties which were, throughout the relevant part of the history of music used as reasons for the aesthetic judgments.

The closest to the concept of preference relevant for this chapter may be found in a study conducted by Müller, where two groups – 16 music experts and 16 music laypersons – were asked to form aesthetic evaluation of musical sequences. The limitation of this study was that the sequences were extremely short (consisting of five successive chords, see Figure 8). Both groups of subjects were presented with five-chord sequences, in which the fifth chord sounded either congruous, ambiguous or incongruous in relation to the harmonic context established by the preceding four chords. The subjects were asked to form a judgment on the harmonic correctness and on the *aesthetic value* of the sequences. Their neurological activity was also measured during the procedure by the EEG.[237]

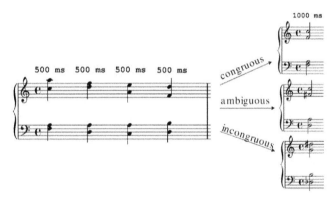

Figure 8: Example of the sequences used in the study, and the three possible ending chords which sound either congruous, ambiguous, or incongruous with the established harmonic context.[238]

---

[237] Mira Müller et al., "Aesthetic Judgments of Music in Experts and Laypersons – An ERP Study," *International Journal of Psychophysiology* 76, no. 1 (2010): 40-51.

[238] The image was acquired from Müller et al., "Aesthetic Judgments of Music in Experts and Laypersons," p. 42.

The results of this study showed that, according to the behavioural measures, experts and laypersons did not show many differences: their judgments on beauty of the sequences did not significantly differ. However, the EEG measures showed that there were clear physiological differences during evaluation making between the experts and laypersons. Several differences between the two groups in the neurological parameters related to the auditory, cognitive and aesthetic processing of the musical sequences (recorded while they were forming judgments) were interpreted by the researchers to indicate, first, that experts invested more effort into preparation for aesthetic judgments than into correctness judgments, and, conversely, that laypersons invested more effort into preparation for the correctness judgement than the beauty judgement task.

Apart from showing that there are certain differences in cognitive and aesthetic processing between music experts and laypersons, it still needs to be worked out exactly what is the significance of the results such as these. The specific results of this study are not very important for the topic of this chapter. The aim of this section was, in fact, to show the examples of the studies conducted so far on music preferences, and to emphasize their scarcity when the concept of preference is understood in a way that would be relevant for the aesthetic judgments, or aesthetic criteria.

Experts versus Laypersons

It should also be noted that, apart from dealing with the aesthetic judgments directly, one aspect of the Müller study is additionally important for the topic of this chapter, namely, the comparison between experts and laypersons. For the dispositionalist view, it is important to see how the musical experts form their judgments and preferences, and it is implicitly understood that their judgments would (sometimes or often) differ from the judgments of laypersons. In any case, it is their judgments that would be taken as relevant for discussing aesthetic criteria. It would be interesting to see whether the factors mentioned by Schaefer and the two theoretical models (LeBlanc's and Hargreaves) equally influence the preferences of music experts and non-experts. The results of Smith and Melara[239] support this possibility. They designed a task in which they manipulated a harmonic progression (consisting of nine chords) and formed a range of six variations starting from the most typical and ending with the least typical chord progression. They then asked the participants – divided into two groups: music experts (music majors and professors) and novices (with six months of music appreciation and theory training) – to rate the 'unusualness', 'complexity', 'interestingness', and 'pleasingness' of each variation. The results showed that both groups perceived the changes of (a)typicality made by the experimenters, evident in the fact that their unusualness, complexity and interestingness ratings increased with the degree of atypicality. The only difference between the two groups was in the pleasingness ratings. Namely, while the experts' pleasingness ratings were proportional to the degree of atypicality, the novices' ratings were in reverse proportion to it. In other words, the novices showed the highest preferences for the most typical chord progressions, while the experts showed the highest preferences for the most atypical progressions.[240]

When faced with differences in preferences or liking ('pleasingness') in cases such as these, it is natural to ask whether it can also be shown that experts and laypersons differ not only in their taste in music, but also in their competence to make judgments about musical pieces. The following section deals with this issue by exploring the differences between experts and non-experts in various capacities involved in listening to music.

---

[239] David J. Smith and Robert J. Melara, "Aesthetic Preference and Syntactic Prototypicality in Music: Tis the Gift to be Simple," *Cognition* 34, no. 3 (1990): 279-298.

[240] *Ibid.*, pp. 286-290.

2.3 Empirical Research on Music Sensitivity

Behavioral Studies

Numerous behavioral studies were conducted which searched for the differences in capacities between musically trained and untrained subjects. I will shortly present the methods of such studies and how they established superiority of musically trained in comparison to untrained subjects in detecting changes in various musical features. In one representative study, Halpern and colleagues devised a same/different discrimination task for pairs of melodies, and tested the difference in performance success in musicians and non-musicians.[241] The participants were presented with pairs of melodies which were either the same or slightly different. The task involved recognizing whether the two melodies are the same or different. This study also examined an additional variable – the age of the participants. The study examined the ability of younger (18-23 years) and older (60-80 years) musicians and non-musicians to discriminate among melodies which differ only in one aspect (rhythm, mode, or contour). The study has shown that musicians perform significantly better than non-musicians, and that age did not show to be a factor with a significant impact.[242]

Another discrimination study explored the influence of quantity of musical training, and the area of musical expertise (voice, percussion instrument, non-percussion instrument) on the perception of musical features.[243] The subjects were divided into three groups: non-musicians with 0-4 years of musical experience, intermediate musicians with 5-7 years of experience, and advanced musicians with 8 or more years of experience. All subjects were presented with pair of short (2.5 seconds) musical sequences. The two sequences in the pair were either identical,

---

[241] Andrea R. Halpern, James C. Bartlett, and Walter Jay Dowling, "Perception of Mode, Rhythm, and Contour in Unfamiliar Melodies: Effects of Age and Experience," *Music Perception: An Interdisciplinary Journal* 15, no. 4 (1998): 335-355.

[242] Halpern et al., "Perception of Mode, Rhythm, and Contour," p. 354.

[243] Irene Kannyo and Caroline M. DeLong, "The Effect of Musical Training on Auditory Perception," *The Journal of the Acoustical Society of America* 130, no. 4 (2011): 24-28.

differed in one aspect (pitch, timber, or rhythm), or differed in two aspects (pitch and timber, pitch and rhythm, or timber and rhythm).[244]

The subjects were given a task: to report whether they hear the difference, and also to recognize the kind of difference. The results showed that the advanced musicians performed the best (with 91.2% performance success), followed by the intermediate groups (85.0% success), and finally the non-musicians (70.0% success). In the area of musical expertise, however, there was no effect on detection of differences in musical features. The researchers concluded that "musical training in any area increases the ability to perceive changes in pitch, timber, and rhythm across unfamiliar auditory sequences."[245]

Apart from suggesting that musical expertise (as opposed to age or the specific area of musical expertise) correlated with better performance, the superiority of musically trained in comparison to non-trained subjects was unambiguously supported and extended by a multitude of other studies, which tested sensitivity to tempo modulations,[246] pitch movements,[247] changes in rhythm and harmony.[248]

It is not surprising that the subjects trained in a certain area such as music have superior detection and differentiation abilities than the inexperienced subjects. In the

---

[244] Kannyo and DeLong, *op. cit.*, p. 27.

[245] *Ibid.*, p. 27-8.

[246] Clifford K. Madsen, "Modulated Beat Discrimination among Musicians and Nonmusicians," *Journal of Research in Music Education* 27, no. 2 (1979): 57-67.

[247] Annemarie Seither Preisler et al., "Tone Sequences With Conflicting Fundamental Pitch and Timbre Changes Are Heard Differently by Musicians and Nonmusicians," *Journal of Experimental Psychology: Human Perception and Performance* 33, no. 3 (2007): 743-51. See also Mark A. Pitt, "Perception of Pitch and Timbre by Musically Trained and Untrained Listeners," *Journal of Experimental Psychology: Human Perception and Performance* 20, no. 5 (1994): 976-986.

[248] Lloyd A. Dawe, John R. Platt, and Ronald J. Racine, "Rhythm Perception and Differences in Accent Weights for Musicians and Nonmusicians," *Perception and Psychophysics* 57, no. 6 (1995): 905-914.

next section, I will present what I believe is a more interesting aspect of the difference between these two groups of subjects.

Neurological Studies

Numerous studies have investigated the neurocognitive basis of differences in performance between experts and non-experts. The studies presented in the next section will offer a few suggestions of some of the underlying mechanisms behind the behavioral differences between musical experts and non-experts. The first study measured whether musicians and non-musicians differ in detecting musical changes both when they are paying attention and when they ignore the musical stimuli. The difference was perceived not only behaviorally, but also in the neurological reactions of the participants.

Superiority of Experts On the Level of Processing

Koelsch and colleagues investigated whether musical expertise influences the automatic neurological detection of changes in the acoustic environment.[249] In their own words, they wanted to determine the effect of long-term musical training on 'pre-attentive acoustic processing', that is, processing without paying attention to the stimuli. The neurological indicator of the automatic (unconscious) detection of change is reflected in a change in the electrical activity of the brain, known as 'mismatch negativity' (MMN). This reaction was associated in the previous research with neurological processes related to pre-attentive detection of change in the auditory input.[250] This means that the MMN reaction is evoked even when the subjects do not

---

[249] Stefan Koelsch, Erich Schröger, and Mari Tervaniemi, "Superior Pre-Attentive Auditory Processing in Musicians," *NeuroReport: For Rapid Communication of Neuroscience Research*, 10, no. 6 (1999): 1309-1313.

[250] The mismatch negativity is known to be a reaction to a change within a sequence of otherwise regular stimuli. A theoretical account on this reaction is that it is evoked by the (possibly unconscious) perception of a violation of regularities of information in the

pay attention to the change in the auditory input. The researchers predicted that this reaction will occur in experts when the impure chords are presented, but not in non-experts, regardless of whether they pay attention to the stimuli or ignore them.[251]

Procedure

The subjects were divided into two groups: experts (professional violinists with more than 12 years of experience) and non-experts (no musical training). None of the subjects had absolute pitch.

Stimuli were pure (sinusoidal) tones. These tones are characteristic for having a single frequency without any harmonics, and are recognizable for sounding very clear, similar to a whistle. During the experimental procedure, brain responses of the participants to the auditory stimuli were recorded by the EEG. Stimuli consisted of two groups: the 'standard' and the 'deviant' stimuli. The standard stimulus was a major chord with a perfect major third. The deviant stimulus was the same chord, only with a slight change in frequency of the third, which makes it a slightly impure chord. This means that the standard and the deviant stimulus differed only in their middle tones.[252]

First block: detection in the pre-attentive state

In the first block, the subjects were instructed to read a book of their choice while the chords were played, and to ignore the auditory stimuli. The subjects were not informed about the differences in the chords. The results showed that in experts, the

---

environment. See Risto Näätänen et al., "Attention and Mismatch Negativity," *Psychophysiology* 30, no. 5 (1993): 436-450. Also see Elvira Brattico et al., "Musical Scale Properties are Automatically Processed in the Human Auditory Cortex," *Brain Research* 1117, no. 1 (2006): 162-174.

[251] Koelsch et al., "Superior Pre-Attentive Auditory Processing in Musicians," p. 1309.

[252] Koelsch et al., *op. cit.*, p. 1310.

deviant stimuli elicited a distinct MMN reaction as opposed to the standard stimuli, as predicted. In non-experts, there was no difference in neurological reactions to pure and impure chords, also as predicted. This indicates that cognitive processing of auditory information did not differ between pure and slightly impure chords in non-musicians. After the first block, the subjects were asked whether they noticed the impure chords, and only six out of eleven experts reported that they did, even though the neurological responses of all experts were equally sensitive to the auditory changes. All non-experts reported that they did not notice the impure chords.[253]

Second block: detection while paying attention

In the second block, the subjects were presented with the same chords. In this block, however, they were *informed* about the existence of deviant stimuli, and were asked to detect them. The purpose of this block was to reveal whether the deviant stimuli were consciously discriminable. The behavioral results showed that experts detected on average 83% of the deviants, while non-musicians detected 13%. They also showed that any participant in the musicians group was able to detect at least 67% of the impure chords, while in the group of non-musicians, six out of eleven detected less than 1% of the impure chords.[254] This confirms the superior ability of experts in auditory discrimination in *attentive* state, suggested by the studies I presented in previous sections.

Additionally, the neurological results replicated the results of the first block. A distinct mismatch reaction was elicited in musicians during only deviant stimuli. More interestingly, the MMN was followed by an additional reaction, namely, the N2b-P3 complex.[255] The N2b-P3 complex is a reaction that usually occurs along with the mismatch reaction, but when attention is directed to the stimuli. This complex is known to reflect higher cognitive processes related to the *conscious* detection and

---

[253] *Ibid.*, pp. 1310-11.

[254] *Ibid.*

[255] *Ibid.*, p. 1312.

evaluation of deviant stimuli.[256] In the second block, non-experts showed a slight mismatch negativity reaction (MMN), but no subsequent N2b-P3 response, in contrast with the experts.[257] Such results confirm that experts possess superior auditory processing when they do not attend the stimuli, but also when they do pay attention to them. In other words, whether the participants ignored or attended to the stimuli, musicians were able to detect more impure chords, while non-musicians were not able to differentiate pure and slightly mistuned chords even when they attended the stimuli.[258]

Third block: replicating the results of the first block

In the third block, the procedure of the first block was repeated, in order to replicate the results of the first block, and to determine whether the second block (when the participants did pay attention to the stimuli) helped non-musicians in transferring the practice of discrimination to the third block, when they were instructed to ignore the stimuli again. The results of the first block were fully replicated: musicians showed an MMN response which did not differ from their response in the first block, while non-musicians again showed no MMN reaction, in spite of the potentially helpful task in the second block. Additionally, identically to the first block, neither experts nor non-experts showed N2b or P3 reactions, confirming that in the third block they managed to ignore the stimuli, and also confirming the role of the N2b-P3 complex in the conscious detection of the stimuli.[259]

---

[256] See Wichian Sittiprapaporn and Jun Soo Kwon, "Brain Electric Microstate and Perception of Simultaneously Audiovisual Presentation," in Artificial Neural Networks – ICANN 2009, 19th International Conference, Limassol, Cyprus, September 14-17, 2009, Proceedings, Part I, p. 346.

[257] Koelsch et al., *op. cit.*, p. 1312.

[258] *Ibid.*

[259] *Ibid.*, p. 1311.

Implications of the Results

These results show several important points. First, they show that musicians are better at detecting certain features in music compared to non-musicians, which is evident in the differences of percentages in the performance success. Second, the neurological data provide even more valuable information. The mismatch reactions show that musicians automatically detect the slightly impure chords even when they ignore them, while the non-musicians do not. This implies that the difference between these two groups of subject occurs already at the automatic processing level. Otherwise, the results could leave an open possibility that the non-musicians also detected the change in musical features, but were perhaps not equipped with sufficient theoretical knowledge to interpret or articulate this information properly. The absence of the mismatch reaction (characteristic of automatic detection) implies that the information about the impure chords did not even enter the non-musicians' cognitive systems. In other words, it is not the case that the non-musicians were unable to interpret or articulate the perceptual information about the impure chord, but rather that they did not even acquire the said information. Third, when the participants did pay attention to the changes in musical stimuli (the second block), non-musicians showed only a slight mismatch reaction, meaning that even when they pay attention to the stimuli, they are still less sensitive to the changes compared to musicians ignoring the stimuli. Finally, the conscious detection reaction (N2b-P3) helps us paint an even richer picture of the differences in cognitive processes between these two groups of subjects. The fact that this reaction was absent in non-musicians even when they attended the stimuli implies that even when the information is automatically registered (shown by the slight MMN reaction), it is not further consciously processed.

In summary, this study demonstrates that musically trained subjects automatically detect differences in auditory input which are undetectable for non-experts, regardless of whether they pay attention to the stimuli or not. Moreover, the results of this study show that the difference between musically trained and untrained subjects goes deeper than the difference in theoretical knowledge or performance success. The cognitive systems of these groups of subjects differently process musical input, both when the input is ignored or attended to.

It is still legitimate to ask whether the cognitive differences are a result of musical training, or whether they can be contributed to some other factors not related to musical training. The following study shows, by testing similar cognitive differences in musicians and non-musicians, how such questions can be examined experimentally.

Expertise and Neuroplasticity

The mismatch response (MMN) and the conscious detection reaction (N2b-P3) found in the Koelsch study are only some of many neurological differences detected between musicians and non-musicians. The study conducted by Bosnyak and colleagues[260] builds on the previous research which reports that musicians exhibit enhancements in certain neurological reactions compared to non-musicians.[261]

Bosnyak and colleagues focus on a specific group of changes in brain activity which reflect the activities of certain populations of neurons in the brain. More precisely, they focus on the 'auditory evoked responses' – the reactions to certain auditory events that are enhanced in musicians. In the psychological literature, these responses are named P1, P2, N1, and N1c.[262] The experimenters were interested in

[260] Daniel J. Bosnyak, Robert A. Eaton, and Larry Evan Roberts, "Distributed Auditory Cortical Representations Are Modified When Non-musicians Are Trained at Pitch Discrimination with 40 Hz Amplitude Modulated Tones," *Cerebral Cortex* 14, no. 10 (2004): 1088-99.

[261] See Koelsch et al., "Superior Pre-Attentive Auditory Processing in Musicians," and also Christo Pantev et al., "Increased Auditory Cortical Representation in Musicians," *Nature* 392 (1998): 811-814.

[262] The names of these reactions refer to the direction (positive vs. negative) of the amplitude of the electromagnetic wave recorded by the EEG, and the time (counted in 100s of milliseconds) passed after the stimulus onset. Thus, P1 amplitude refers to the most positive peak of the wave which occurs between 40 milliseconds and 110 millisecond after stimulus onset, and P2 amplitude refers to the most positive peak occurring between 120 milliseconds and 200 milliseconds. Similarly, N1 amplitude refers to the most negative peak occurring between 90 milliseconds and 120 milliseconds after stimulus onset, and N1c was defined as

testing whether these enhancements in musicians are a result of neuroplasticity induced by training and practice, or whether they result from some other factors. The mere difference in these neurological components between musicians and non-musicians is not sufficient to rule out the possibility that the enhancements result from earlier influences, or even a genetic code associated with development of auditory cortex, which subsequently influences the decision to train musically. Thus, Bosnyak and colleagues designed an experiment to assess neuroplasticity directly, by measuring the participants' neurological responses (P1, P2, N1, and N1c) before, during, and after the participants' training at acoustic discriminations.[263]

Procedure

Eight subjects, graduate students, participated in the study which consisted of two test sessions, and 18 sessions of auditory discrimination training. None of the subjects had prior musical training or formal musical education.[264]

Preliminary session (for selecting the appropriate stimuli)

Before the experiment, a preliminary session was conducted in which the discrimination ability of the participants was measured. On each trial, a 'standard stimulus' (S1) and a 'comparison stimulus' (S2) were presented to the participants. The stimuli were the same in 50% of the trials, and the subjects were asked to indicate whether they believed the tones they heard had the same or different frequency. The comparison stimuli were adjusted to differ from the standard more or less according to their performance. The purpose of the preliminary session was to select the stimuli that will be used in the experiment, adjusted individually for each subject, so that the

---

the most negative peak occurring between 120 milliseconds and 180 milliseconds. See Antoine Shahin et al., "Enhancement of Neuroplastic P2 and N1c Auditory Evoked Potentials in Musicians," *Journal of Neuroscience* 23, no. 13 (2003): 5545-5552.

[263] Bosnyak et al., "Distributed Auditory Cortical Representations Are Modified," p. 1089.

[264] *Ibid.*

difficulty is at the medium level, i.e., that the probability for correct answer is 0.5, and also to make the subjects familiar with the pure tones used in the rest of the experiment.[265]

Two test sessions

The first testing ('Test 1') was conducted before the training series, and the second test ('Test 2') was given after the training series, approximately 18 days later. The test sessions consisted of three blocks, and each block contained 360 trials. Similarly to the already presented Halpern's behavioral study with melodies, the task was recognizing whether the two tones are of the same or different frequency. The subjects were not informed of the correctness of their answers.[266]

The three blocks involved three different sets of stimuli. In one block the 'standard stimulus' (S1) was 2.0 kHz. The 'comparison frequencies' (S2) varied from 2.0 to 2.1 kHz. This set of stimuli was named the 'trained set' because it is the set used in the training sessions.[267] In the remaining two blocks of the test, S1 stimuli were either 1.8 kHz or 2.2 kHz, while the S2 stimuli were 0-100 Hz higher. The second and third stimuli sets were 'control' sets, used to determine whether changes detected after training occurred specifically for the frequencies the subjects were trained to discriminate (2.0 kHz), or whether they generalized to other frequencies as well.[268]

Each trial was designed so that the participants listen to the standard stimulus first, and then after a 0.5 seconds pause to the comparison stimulus. In one half of the trials, the comparison stimulus (S2) was the same as the standard stimulus (S1). In other half, S2 was one of six different comparison tones, which varied from being 2 Hz to 60 Hz higher than S1. The frequencies of the comparison stimuli were selected

---

[265] *Ibid.*, p. 1089.

[266] *Ibid.*

[267] *Ibid.*, p. 1089.

[268] *Ibid.*, pp. 1089-90.

by the authors of the study according to the participants' previous success, so that the participants were expected to detect two of them in at least 50% of the trials, and the other two in less than 50% of the trials. When hearing both stimuli, the participants reported whether they believed they were same or different.[269]

Frequencies involved in the test sessions were identical before and after training, in order to allow the researchers comparison of the participants' performance.[270]

Training sessions

Over the course of roughly 18 days, the researchers conducted fifteen training sessions. They were similar to the test sessions, with a few alterations. First, only the stimulus set in which S1 was 2.0 kHz was trained, and not all three stimuli groups. Second, the participants received feedback about the correctness of their judgments. Similarly to the test sessions, the comparison stimulus was 2.0 kHz on the 'same' trials, and switched between the six higher frequencies on the 'different' trials. Third, the researchers included an 'adaptive procedure' after each session in which the participants performed without error on more than one of the comparison frequencies. The adaptive procedure consisted in removing the highest comparison frequency (the easiest one to be detected) and replacing it with the frequency which was expected to yield the 50% probability of the correct judgement. In other words, the researchers gradually increased the difficulty of the task with the improvement of the participants.[271]

---

[269] *Ibid.*, p. 1090.

[270] *Ibid.*, p. 1089.

[271] *Ibid.*, p. 1090.

Results

Behavioral results

Gradual performance improvement

The results showed that overall performance of the participants improved significantly since the first test session, and this improvement occurred *gradually* throughout the training series. It can be observed on the graph that performance first improved rapidly after the first test session (Test 1), and then more gradually afterwards, until the closing test session (Test 2) – see Figure 9A.[272]

Before/after improvement and generalization

When the results were observed for each stimulus set separately, comparing performance success before (Test 1) and after (Test 2) the training series showed a significant before/after improvement for all three stimulus sets. It was found that the participants showed improvement in discriminating in all three sets of stimuli, however, the improvement was higher for the trained stimuli (2.0 kHz) than for the untrained stimuli (1.8 kHz and 2.2 kHz).[273] Even though the subjects were more successful in the tasks with the trained stimuli, these results also implicate the improvement generalized to the stimuli which the subjects were not trained in – see Figure 9B.

---

[272] *Ibid.*, p. 1092.

[273] *Ibid.*, p. 1092.

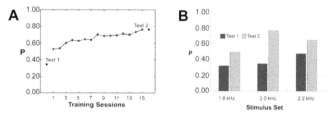

Figure 9: Behavioral performance of the participants:[274]
(A) The performance success on the opening (Test 1) and closing (Test 2) test sessions, and over 15 sessions of the training series. Data are shown for the trained (2.0 kHz) stimulus set.
(B) Performance for three stimulus groups (1.8 kHz, 2.0 kHz, and 2.2 kHz) before and after the training series.

Precision in discriminating

An additional effect of the training was the increase in precision. Discrimination thresholds decreased from before the training significantly, meaning that, after the training, the participants were able to notice smaller differences between tones than before training. For example, prior to training, for the trained (2.0 kHz) stimuli set, the participants were able to discern between tones differing in 20.2 Hz, while after the training they were able to discriminate between tones differing in as little as 9.3 Hz.[275] In other words, not only were the participants better in terms of how often they gave correct answers to the same differences in frequency, but also in how small the difference they were able to recognize.

Long-term retention of the changes

In addition, six participants returned for a 'retention test' two months after the last test session. They were only tested for the trained stimulus set (2.0 kHz). Their performance success at retention (63%) was lower than at the end of the training (75%) but still significantly higher than in the first testing (32%).[276]

---

[274] The image was acquired from Bosnyak et al., "Distributed Auditory Cortical Representations Are Modified," p. 1092.

[275] Ibid., p. 1092.

[276] Ibid., p. 1092.

Neurological results

The neurological reactions were recorded by the EEG in the two test sessions as well as in training sessions 3 and 13. The aim of the measurement was to determine the possible changes in the P1, P2, N1 and N1c activity before, during, and after the training series.[277]

Only two out of four components measured by the EEG showed changes relevant for the hypothesis of the experiment. The reactions named P2 and N1c complemented the behavioral results in that they were significantly enhanced after the training series. The other two reactions (P1 and N1) did not seem to be affected by the training. [278]

The training resulted in an enhancement of amplitudes of the P2 and N1c reactions. The differences before and after training in P2 and N1c reaction for each of the three stimulus sets are shown in Figure 10A and 10B, respectively. As the graph shows, these differences were largest for the trained stimuli, but enhancement generalized to the control sets, similarly to the generalized improvement in behavioral performance.[279]

Gradual enhancement

It was also found that the training sessions lead to a *gradual* enhancement of the P2 and the N1c reaction over the training series. The gradual enhancement of P2 and N1c over sessions is shown in Figure 10C starting with Test 1, through the training sessions 3 and 13, and ending with Test 2. Figure 10C also displays the insignificant changes in P1 and N1 responses, for which it seems that the training sessions had no

---

[277] *Ibid.*, p. 1090.

[278] *Ibid.*, p. 1093.

[279] *Ibid.*

effect. The amplitudes of these two measures even seemed to decrease after training, but not significantly.[280]

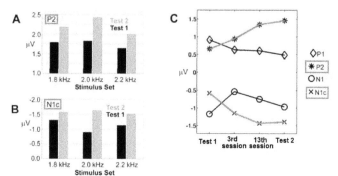

Figure 10. Neurological changes in components P2 and N1c:[281]
(A) Changes in amplitude of P2 before and after training for each of the three stimuli groups;
(B) Changes in amplitude of N1c before and after training for each of the three stimuli groups;
(C) Gradual enhancement of P2 (the positive amplitude becomes increasingly higher) and N1c (the negative amplitude rises toward even more negative values), confirming the neuroplasticity hypothesis. Changes in P1 and N1 did not occur according to the experimenters' hypothesis for these reactions.

Robustness of the results

Bosnyak and colleagues note that the P2 enhancement effect resulting from auditory training was already shown in the literature. It was already described in an earlier study which used the same methods as the ones Bosnyak and colleagues used.[282] In addition, the same enhancement was found in other studies in which musically untrained participants were trained to discriminate temporal properties of speech

---

[280] *Ibid.*, p. 1093.

[281] The image was acquired from Bosnyak et al., "Distributed Auditory Cortical Representations Are Modified," p. 1093.

[282] See Robert A. Eaton and Larry E. Roberts, "Effect of Spectral Frequency Discrimination on Auditory Transient and Steady State Responses in Humans," *Society for Neuroscience Abstracts* 29 (1999): 156.15.

signals,[283] or to detect pitch deviants in a short stream of pitch stimuli.[284] The finding of the P2 enhancement effect thus seems to be well supported. On the other hand, Bosnyak and colleagues note that enhancement of the N1c component by auditory discrimination training has not been found so far, and their study is thus the first to provide demonstration of the N1c effect.[285]

Implications of the Results

Bosnyak and colleagues rely on the reports of the previous research that musicians exhibit enhancements in certain neurological reactions compared to non-musicians. They tested whether these enhancements are a direct result of musical training. Their results show that both performance success and the P2 and N1c amplitudes (usually higher in musicians than non-musicians) were significantly higher after the training series than before. The finding that both behavioral and neurological measures *gradually* increased over the course of the musical training series confirm the hypothesis that the neurocognitive enhancements are indeed a result of neuroplasticity induced by the musical training. The hypothesis is additionally confirmed by the result that the performance success as well as the enhancement of the neurological reactions both generalized to stimuli which the subjects were not trained in, excluding the alternative explanation that the subjects become accustomed to perform only the tasks on the trained stimuli. This finding fits with the previously discussed behavioral results of the Kannyo and DeLong study which shows that musical training in any area, regardless of the instrument learned, increases the ability of the subjects to detect changes in pitch, rhythm, and timber in novel auditory input.[286]

---

[283] Kelly Tremblay et al., "Central Auditory Plasticity: Changes in the N1-P2 Complex After Speech-Sound Training," *Ear and Hearing* 22, no. 2 (2001):79-90.

[284] Mercedes Atienza, Jose L. Cantero, and Elena Dominguez-Marin, "The Time Course of Neural Changes Underlying Auditory Perceptual Learning," *Learning and Memory* 9, no. 3 (2002): 138-150.

[285] Bosnyak et al., *op. cit.*, p. 1097.

[286] Kannyo and DeLong, *op. cit.*, p. 27-8. See also Section 2.3 of this chapter.

To conclude, the results of this study indicate that the enhancement of the P2 and the N1c component in musically trained compared to untrained subjects most probably is the result of neuroplasticity induced by training. The demonstration of the neuroplasticity of at least some neurocognitive enhancements is a significant result in that it emphasizes the importance of practice and training for the neurocognitive differences correlated with the performance success.

This study also showed that the neurological differences *de facto* mirror some of the capacities by which musical experts differ from non-experts, which is methodologically relevant for the topic of this chapter, in that it shows that the capacities by which experts and non-expert differ can be physiologically tested, which brings additional valuable objective and precisely measured data into the discussion.

Conclusion of the Second Chapter

The aim of this chapter was to show how even the highly abstract and normative concept of value can be related to the results of empirical research. Not any aesthetic theory, however, is suitable to allow for this kind of connection. Most of the philosophical part of the chapter focused on the modified version of Hume's dispositionalist aesthetic theory. The dispositionalist approach to aesthetic value is best fitted for the project carried out in this chapter. I proposed that we should understand the existence of a systematic practice of aesthetic appreciation of musical works as *ratio cognoscendi* of a specific kind of value, which we might posit to be musical value, epistemically unavailable through other means. Conversely, musical value as an objective property of a musical work is to be understood as *ratio essendi* of the mentioned systematic practice, a specific – aesthetic – relation of a multitude of subjects toward a certain type of artefacts. The philosophical part of this chapter, thus, aimed to show that the dispositionalist view in itself contains a conceptual bridge between the normative concept of value (which is interesting for the aesthetics and philosophy of music) and the descriptive concepts related to the subjective responses (which are being investigated in the empirical research).Thus, if we define musical value dispositionally: as being suitable to be appreciated and preferred by the subjects qualified to make the proper judgement, the objective properties of the musical works are thus conceptually connected to the subjective responses of the listeners. These subjective responses are in turn available to be experimentally examined.

Differences Between the Perceiving Subjects

An important aspect of the dispositionalist aesthetics is the claim that there are important differences between the perceiving subjects – not all subjects are equally qualified to make proper aesthetic judgments. The empirical evidence presented in the experimental part of the chapter showed that there are differences between musically trained and untrained subjects.

Superior Performance of the Musically Trained Subjects

First, this chapter presents evidence that already in very simple tasks concerning the detection, recognition, or differentiation of isolated musical elements there are differences between the perceiving subjects, and that trained musicians are better at detecting certain features in music compared to non-musicians, which is evident in the differences of the performance success between these two groups.

Differences at the Processing Level

Second, the results also provide evidence that trained musicians automatically detect differences in auditory information which are undetectable for non-musicians, regardless of whether they pay attention to the stimuli or not. This provides evidence not only of behavioral differences (performance success in the detection tasks), but also of different ways of processing musical information. The neurological results thus provide a more thorough insight into the difference between musically trained and untrained subjects. They show that the difference between musically trained and untrained subjects goes deeper than the difference in theoretical knowledge or performance success, and supplement our notion of expertise so that it does not consist only in formal education or experience, but also in a way of processing musical information. The cognitive systems of these groups of subjects differently process musical input, both when the input is ignored or attended to. This implies that the difference between these two groups of subject occurs already at the automatic processing level. The absence of certain neurological reactions in the untrained subjects implies that some of the perceptual information concerning musical features does not even enter their cognitive systems. Thus, in at least some cases, the difference between trained and untrained subjects is not a matter of interpreting or articulating the perceptual information, but instead a matter of ability to acquire the information at all.

The Role of Musical Training

The studies presented in this chapter also show that at least some of the differences between musically trained and untrained subjects are a result of musical training. This is supported, first, by the finding that performance success in detecting of the previously musically untrained subjects was significantly higher after the training series than before. Second, the neurological reactions that are usually enhanced in musicians in comparison with laypersons also enhanced significantly in these subjects after they were being trained in distinguishing certain musical features. Third, the finding that both behavioral and neurological measures *gradually* increased over the course of the musical training series confirm the hypothesis that the neurocognitive enhancements are indeed a result of neuroplasticity induced by the musical training. Finally, the hypothesis of neuroplasticity is additionally confirmed by the result that the performance success as well as the enhancement of the neurological reactions both generalized even to the stimuli which the subjects were not trained to differentiate. All of these conclusions emphasize the significance of musical training for being able to detect and recognize certain features or changes in music.

Support for Dispositionalism

The evidence of the differences between the musically trained and untrained subjects supports one of the crucial claims of the dispositionalist view. Without the differences between the subjects, it is difficult for the dispositionalists to explain how come music listeners differ in their preferences toward musical works if the aesthetic value inheres in the works themselves and is reflected on the listeners' reactions and preferences. If aesthetic value inheres in the works, the listeners should agree in their judgments regarding which musical works are more valuable than others. As is widely known, such consensus does not exist. If the subjects differ, however, in their capacities to detect and recognize features of musical works, their differences in preferences could in principle be traced to the differences in capacities which are in the basis of, or at least influence their preferences. If, say, a musical work possesses complex and original interplay of certain musical elements, and requires focused attention and accuracy in hearing in order to take notice of these relationships, then the listener who is not able to recognize such relationships might also be unable to understand and recognize the value of the work as a whole. The aesthetic judgement and preference of such listener would then differ from the preference of the listener trained to take notice of such relationships.

Limitations

We should, however, be cautious when inferring further implications from the results of these studies. A couple of limitations of the significance of these results should be noted. The first limitation concerns the scope of the capacities tested. Most of the studies on musical sensitivity focused only on one type of simple task, such as whether the two stimuli are same or different, or what kind of difference was made to the stimuli. Further, the stimuli used were either short musical sequences, or even isolated musical elements such as short melodies or chord progressions. In the Bosnyak training study, only sensitivity to isolated frequencies was tested. It is thus definitely premature to generalize the superiority of trained over the untrained subjects in overall comprehension of musical works, even though it seems that if they are superior in performing simpler tasks, it should follow that they would perform better in the more complex tasks as well. For a more realistic assessment, many other capacities would need to be tested, such as memory, recognition of certain relationships within music, and other more complex capacities. Also, the stimuli involved in the experiments would need to be more diverse, of larger scale, and more similar to the actual musical works. Finally, the tasks involved would need to be more complex and diverse as well, also more resembling to the process of actual aesthetic appreciation of musical works.

The second limitation of the significance of the results presented here concerns the relevance of the tested capacities for making aesthetic judgments. The capacities tested concern accuracy or precision in detecting certain features in music. It is not clear whether these capacities are necessary or sufficient conditions for being qualified to make proper aesthetic judgments, and also whether there are some other qualities, perhaps specifically related to taste, that cannot be measured by the

116

presented methods. The relationships between such measurable capacities and the supposedly 'good taste' need to be elaborated further.

This is connected to the third limitation, already mentioned in the Section 2.2 which presents empirical work on musical preferences. Both systematizing theoretical models and the particular empirical studies on musical preferences are too problematic to be used for the purposes of this chapter, as well as on their own. Even if they were methodologically sound and provided significant results, the conception of music preference is not the one relevant for aesthetic judgments. By music preference they refer either to the short-term, almost momentary judgement of 'liking' the musical work, or to choosing a musical work as a personal favorite. The only study which involves the relevant subjective judgement is the study presented above, conducted by Müller (see Section 2.2), in which musicians and laypersons were required to make aesthetic judgments on five chord harmonic progressions. The relevance of Müller's results is, however, also limited due to the fact that the overall implications of the study are unclear: the results showed that the two groups of subjects did not differ in their aesthetic judgments concerning the sequences, but differed in the neurological processes recorded while they were making these judgments.

Suggestions for Further Research

Despite the limitations, the studies presented in this chapter are important for showing that at least some of the musically-related capacities of the perceiving subjects can be objectively measured and compared. These studies also present us with the methods for performing such measurements. They show how the question of musical expertise can be empirically approached, and with further research eventually the question of the criteria of musical value might be reached as well. The conclusions of this chapter should, thus, be taken only as a part of an early phase of the empirical research of musical value, which should be complemented from various other sides – such as using large-scale musical works, assigning different types of behavioral tasks, measuring many other neurocognitive responses, etc.

These results can be connected to the problem of aesthetic value of musical works through establishing correlations between differences in capacities and in preferences. One way to test these correlations would be to test both capacities and preferences before and after training, similarly to the method of the Bosnyak study, and observe whether the capacities and the preferences change with any significant degree of correlation.

Chapter 3 – Emotions in Music

In contemporary analytic aesthetics of music there is much of interest regarding the expressive aspect of music. It seems that philosophical works about music focus mostly on the expressiveness of music, and in general on the relationship between music and the emotions. This interest in the emotions in music is understandable, since undoubtedly both trained and untrained listeners speak of music as if it expresses emotions, and it is common to describe music by words referring to emotions. It is then natural to ask what lies behind such speech about music, and what constitutes the basis of musical expressiveness, and of our experience of music as expressive. At first, given that music is not a sentient being, i.e., it is not someone who could experience emotions, it seems unclear how propositions about sad, cheerful, melancholic music make sense. On the other hand, such way of talking do not seem paradoxical. Even the music theorists who do not consider emotions to be essential for music allow that this is a natural way to speak about music, and that our experience, and perhaps even understanding of music might be impoverished, were we to abandon such way of speaking.

There were several notable attempts to render such ways of talking and experience of music more coherent. These attempts constitute different views on the expressiveness of music. As we will see, some of them attempt to explain musical expressiveness by appealing to the feelings of the composer (or the performer), some by appealing to the emotions experienced by the listeners, and some by focusing only on the properties of the music itself. These views, aside from explaining musical expressiveness differently, differ also in their views on another relationship between music and the emotions, tightly related to expressiveness, namely, the ability of music to arouse emotions in the listeners. Some of the accounts of expressiveness imply that music does arouse genuine emotions in the listeners, even though they may not be the same emotions that are expressed by the musical work. Other accounts deny this possibility, and replace ordinary emotions mentioned in other theories with 'musical emotions', or 'quasi-emotions'. In short, there are several way to understand musical expressiveness, musical influence on human emotions, and the relationship between the expressiveness and the arousal of the emotions.

In this chapter, some of the most influential theories of musical expressiveness will be considered, followed by a discussion of an influential account of musically induced emotions that counters some implicit assumptions of those theories. After that, I will consider how the experimental research in music psychology relates to these claims, and whether some of them can be supported or refuted by the results of these experiments.

1 Philosophical Theories on the Emotions in Music

1.1 The Expression Theory: Emotions of the Composer

The first view explains musical expressiveness as an expression of the emotions experienced by the composer. This is the most natural approach, because if anybody is "responsible" for the emotions in a musical piece, it is its author. According to this view, expressiveness of music arises from the artists' expressing their emotions through the act of composition. These emotions are recognized and responded to.[287] There are several versions of this view, but I believe it is not necessary to go into details of each of them, since the crucial objections which justify rejection of this view apply to its fundamental assumptions, and therefore to all the different versions of the view. One line of criticism consists of empirical objections. It is argued that we do not actually know what the composers felt, and what, if anything, they attempted to express by the musical piece. From what we do know about their work methods, composing, especially in the case of large-scale works, extends to long periods of time, and generally requires methodical and technical thinking rather than the passionate outpouring we are prone to imagine. Further, even when composers do wish to express their emotions through the musical work, their intentions are not necessarily fulfilled. This is particularly so with inept composers – Davies mentions Ernest Chausson and Henri Duparc as examples.[288] This demonstrates that the mere intention on the part of the composers to express emotion is not sufficient for their work to be characterized as expressive. Thus, the expression theory does not offer a good explanation of the expressiveness of musical works.

Even setting aside these objections, this view faces conceptual obstacles as well, namely, the problem of understanding how composers "place" their emotions into the work, on listening to which they are then recognized and understood. The

---

[287] Stephen Davies, *Musical Meaning and Expression*, Ithaca and London: Cornell UP, 1994, pp. 168-70.

[288] Davies, *op. cit.*, p. 172.

expression theory supposes that the expressiveness of a process is transmitted to the product of that process, and that the expressiveness of an action is apparent in the product of that action.[289] The expression theory needs to provide further explanations concerning the transmission of expressiveness to the artwork, in order to be able to clarify the phenomenon of expressiveness. One possible explanation could be that the composers do not "pour" their emotions directly into the music, but instead they choose the musical elements and their combinations which fit the emotions through their own inherent expressive character: minor and diminished chords are more suitable to expressing sorrow and melancholy, while major chords and faster tempo are more suitable to expressions of joy and excitement.[290] But even though this refinement of the theory is plausible and is consonant with musical practice, the explanation itself goes against the expression theory, since it suggests that the expressiveness of the musical work lies in the musical material itself, rather than in the emotions of the composer.

---

[289] *Ibid.*, p. 173.

[290] Stephen Davies, "Contra the Hypothetical Persona in Music", in Mette Hjort and Sue Laver (eds.), *Emotion and the Arts*, New York: Oxford UP, 1997, pp. 95-6.

1.2 The Arousal Theory

According to another popular theory, that a musical work expresses an emotion consists in the work's arousing that emotion in the listener. For example, the sadness of a piece of music consists in its power to evoke sadness in the listener. Music's expressiveness consists in its power to move people.[291] This is a natural approach as well, because it is always the listener who attributes emotions to the music.

The first question that we need to ask is why the emotion is attributed to the musical work given that it is felt by the listener. One of the more convincing answers is that, even though the emotions expressed belong to the listener, the expressiveness is correctly attributed to the music as a dispositional property because responses to music have an interpersonal validity. This interpersonal validity is based on the fact that music affects human emotions due to its possessing certain properties. In principle, there should be underlying rules or laws governing what kinds of properties produce what kind of aesthetic responses, though in practice we might not be able to abstract such rules. Therefore, according to the arousal theory, music evokes emotions in the listeners due to its possessing certain properties (describable in musical terms without reference to the listener's response).[292] It is important for proponents of this theory to include the features of the musical work into the account of expressiveness, in order to stress that the relevant response of the listeners must arise from an experience of certain types of features in the musical work itself (thus the relevant experience should involve thoughts about the particular work, assuming knowledge of wider musical considerations, such as style, and a sensitivity to the history of musical practice), thereby excluding cases where music is merely the occasion for a response, e.g. where "a father is saddened by a work because it was his dead son's favorite, though normally the piece would be described as happy".[293] This is an important condition because it helps to explain various situations in which music expressive of some emotion fails to arouse that emotion in the listener, arousing instead a different one or, indeed, no emotion at all. Various factors that can interfere with the arousal or

---

[291] Davies, *Musical Meaning and Expression*, pp. 184-5.

[292] *Ibid.*, p. 187.

[293] *Ibid.*

bring about the listener's lack of a response (such as failure to focus on the music) do not change the fact that the musical work is expressive.[294]

There are in fact many cases in which there is a mismatch between the emotion attributed to the music and the emotion aroused in the listener. Even though sad music does sometimes or often move its listeners to sadness, there are also cases in which we wish to say that the music expresses sadness though it does not move the listener to sadness despite the listener's careful attention to the music and the lack of possible intervening factors mentioned by the arousal theory. It could be that the listener feels nothing, or that she responds by some other emotion than the expressed one. Cases of a mismatch between the listener's response (if any) and the expressive character of the musical piece are too common to be ignored, and according to many philosophers, fatal for the arousal theory.[295] It seems that the emotions expressed in musical works and the emotions aroused in the listeners are not connected with a regularity which would suggest that the expressiveness can be explained and analyzed in terms of the arousal. Even though this theory has undergone something of a revival in recent years, and has been refined by the contemporary authors, it still retains this fundamental problem.[296]

---

[294] *Ibid.*, pp. 188-9.

[295] *Ibid.*, pp. 194-5., referring to R. T. Allen, "The Arousal and Expression of Emotion by Music," *British Journal of Aesthetics* 30, no. 1 (1990): 57-61.

[296] Davies, *Musical Meaning and Expression*, pp. 198-9. Also see Donald Callen, "The Sentiment in Musical Sensibility," *Journal of Aesthetics and Art Criticism* 40 (1982): 381-393.; Peter Mew, "The Expression of Emotion in Music," *British Journal of Aesthetics* 25 (1985): 33-42.; Peter Mew, "The Musical Arousal of Emotions," *British Journal of Aesthetics* 25 (1985): 357-361.; John Nolt, "Expression and Emotions," *British Journal of Aesthetics* 21 (1981): 139-150.; Stanley Speck, "Arousal Theory' Reconsidered," *British Journal of Aesthetics* 28 (1988): 40-47.

1.3 Emotion Characteristics in Appearances

Davies holds that all the arguments which speak against the expression theory and the arousal theory provide support to his own view: that the expressiveness lies in the music itself, that it inheres in the properties of the sound, and that it is therefore independent of the emotions of both the composer and the listener.

This view, called by Davies "appearance emotionalism", holds that the musical material itself can be literally expressive by virtue of presenting to audition sounds which possess 'emotion-characteristics'. The sound itself is endowed with such characteristics. Music is sad-sounding in much the way that the weeping willow, or the tragedy mask, is sad-looking. If hearing music's expressiveness requires imagination, it does not require more of it than is needed to see the weeping willow as downhearted, or face masks as having human expressions. Music is heard as expressive due to what Peter Kivy calls an "animating tendency", the natural mode in which humans experience the world.[297]

Davies develops his view by describing the way that the words naming emotions function in language. In their primary use, these words refer to experiencing emotions. However, there are other uses of emotion terms which do not involve reference to experiencing emotions, but retain a direct connection to their primary use, for example, when we speak about dispositions toward feeling emotions: we might describe a person as sad, meaning not that they feel sad now, but that they are, more often than other people, disposed toward that feeling. These uses of emotion words, Davies continues, have no application to music since music is non-sentient – it cannot experience emotions.[298]

There is, however, also a secondary use of emotion terms, which has no reference to the experience of emotions. This use refers to the emotion characteristics in appearances themselves: the character of a person's appearance, face, voice, or bearing, are often described by using emotion terms, and by this we do not mean to speak about the experience of the person we are describing, but to the way she or her

---

[297] Davies, "Contra the Hypothetical Persona in Music", p. 97.

[298] Davies, *Musical Meaning and Expression*, pp. 221-2.

face, voice, etc. *appears* to us. This, according to Davies, is the use we rely on when we speak about the emotional properties of music.[299] What Davies wants to emphasize by this distinction between the primary and the secondary use of emotion terms is that they have a common, unproblematic use that does not involve even implicit reference to any person's experienced emotions. His theory aims to explain why describing music as cheerful, sad, etc. does not seem paradoxical, even though music is not something that can experience emotions.[300]

There is, of course, a connection between the emotion characteristics in appearance and the experienced emotions: the behavior or look that we describe as having emotion characteristics in appearance are the same as as the behavior and look that characteristically and naturally do express experienced emotions. Thus it is not difficult to see why the meanings of emotion terms have been extended to this secondary use.[301]

Primary or natural expressions of emotions are the behaviors we recognize as possessing expressive import without knowing anything of someone's propositional attitudes, the objects of those attitudes, or the emotions of the person we assign the emotion to.[302] Not all emotions have natural, primary expressions (for example, the so-called "higher" emotions such as hope, pride, embarrassment, envy, etc.), and therefore they do not have the corresponding emotion characteristics in appearance either. This is the reason Davies believes that the range of emotions that can be heard in music is limited to the emotions that have recognizable behavioral expressions. He adds, however, that music can express some cognitively complex emotions even though they lack characteristic behavioral expression, by presenting the "appearance of a pattern of feelings through the order of its expressive development," through a

---

[299] *Ibid.*, pp. 222-3.

[300] *Ibid.*, p. 224.

[301] *Ibid.*

[302] *Ibid.*, p. 225.

longer musical section. If the outline of the pattern is sufficiently distinct, it may compensate for the lack of a behavioral expression of the given emotion.[303]

These "expressive appearances", as Davies names them, are the "emergent properties of the things to which they are attributed." In the case of music, the emotion we attribute to the musical piece is the emergent property of the sounds of the musical work. It is presented in the musical work. There is no need for describing, representing, symbolizing, or other kinds of denoting which would connect the musical expressiveness to occurrent emotions, because the expressive character of the music resides within the music itself.[304] The criterion of whether the music possesses an emotional property is given in the appearance itself, i.e. in the music as heard.[305]

Davies still needs to explain in what way music can resemble human manifestations of emotions. He believes that the expressiveness of music depends for the most part on the resemblance between the dynamic character of music and human behavior, movement, bearing, etc. rather than, as someone might think, on the resemblance to the vocal expressions of human emotions. Motion is heard in music, and this motion presents emotion characteristics, just as movements give emotional character to someone's gait or walk.[306] Davies adds that music is heard and described in spatial terms, and that there is movement between the notes, and it is rhythm, meter, tempo, and melody that generate the experience of motion across this space. Also important for the depth or volume in music is its texture, in the sense of notes being placed densely or sparsely, forming a thick or thin music texture, respectively. Richer texture, such as in an orchestral piece, provides more depth and power that a solo violin could not achieve. Register, loudness, softness of sound also contribute to music having a spatial effect.[307] It should then come as no surprise, continues Davies, that music is described constantly in terms primarily used to denote space, movement,

---

[303] *Ibid.*, pp. 225-6, 263.

[304] *Ibid.*, p. 228.

[305] Stephen Davies, "The Expression of Emotion in Music," *Mind* 89 (1980), p. 70.

[306] Davies, *Musical Meaning and Expression*, p. 229.

[307] *Ibid.*, p. 232.

and action: rushing, hesitant, vivacious, dragging, etc.[308] The movement in music is not heard as random, but rather as teleological: "Notes other than tonic are heard as drawn toward it, with the strength of the attraction depending (...) on [the note's] distance from the tonic."[309] Similarly, chords are comparatively tense or relaxed (discordant or concordant) in relation to the tonic chord. As a result, the motion of music "corresponds to an experience of increasing or diminishing tension, push and pull, (...) with closure achieved at the arrival of the final tonic."[310]

These features of musical movement draw attention of the listener to the relevant similarities with human behavior. Musical movement invites attention to expressiveness, because, just like human behavior (and unlike random processes), it "displays order and purposiveness, and provides a sense of unity." We recognize in the progress of music a logic, in the sense that what we hear is not fully determined by what preceded, but still arises naturally from it. Musical movement is thus more similar to human behavior than to random movement, or to the fully determined movements of non-human mechanisms. Most importantly, this feature of music arises from the characteristics of the musical material itself, and not solely from the knowledge that it is humans that have shaped those materials.[311]

It should be noted that, unlike the other two theories of musical expressiveness (the expression and the arousal theory) Davies' theory has more similarity to the theories of meaning in music. His theory could, in fact, be understood as a more elaborated version of the referentialist account of emotional meaning in music, according to Meyer's classification of theories of musical meaning (see Chapter 1, Section 1.3). Instead of only stating the correlations between musical elements and particular emotions, Davies attempts to explain the origin of these correlations. He insists that it is our *experience* of musical works that is similar to our experience of the human behavior perceived as expressive of emotions. The analogy resides in the

---

[308] *Ibid.*, p. 234.

[309] *Ibid.*, p. 236.

[310] *Ibid.*, p. 236.

[311] *Ibid.*, p. 229.

manner in which music and behavior are experienced, rather than being based on some symbolic relation between particular parts and bits of each of them.[312]

Davies claims that this theory is superior to other accounts of musical expressiveness for a number of reasons. First, it allows that expressiveness is a property of music that is always publicly evidenced and directly manifested, which is in accord with our way of experiencing expressiveness in music. Second, this theory does not rely on a connection between musical expressiveness and someone's occurrent emotions or psychological or cognitive state. Third, it involves an attribution of expressiveness that has a familiar use in nonmusical contexts.[313]

In spite of these claims, Davies's view was criticized by the proponents of other theories for conflating, as Jenefer Robinson formulates the objection, "the possession of emotional qualities such as sadness and cheerfulness by music, and emotional *expressiveness* in music". Robinson clarifies this important distinction by exploiting an interesting remark by Peter Kivy: "[Kivy] remarks in passing that Telemann wrote 'yards and yards of mournful music' which is not *moving*. It is presumably mournful in Kivy's view because it resembles mournful human vocal or behavioral expressions and/or because it has some conventional marks of musical mournfulness, but at the same time it is not *expressive*, and because it is not expressive it does not move me: it does not evoke any emotion in me".[314] This is a flat denial of Davies's central claim as counter-intuitive. Thus, some musical piece may have, say, a sad character (because the musical movements in it resemble human gestures which would be perceived as sad) without being expressive at all. It could be perceived, for example, as banal.

As we can see, each of these theories faces serious difficulties. Here some clarifications might be useful, by disentangling several important relationships between music and the emotions, that are apparently considered identical, or necessarily connected by some of these theories, without it being at all evident that

---

[312] *Ibid.*, p. 239.

[313] *Ibid.*, pp. 239-40.

[314] Jenefer Robinson, *Deeper than Reason* (Oxford: Clarendon Press, 2005), pp. 309-10.

this is indeed so. First, whether the *composer* (or performer) intended to express his or her own emotion in creating (or performing) a musical piece is a separate issue from whether the musical piece is heard as expressive of that emotion. In other words, expression of emotion on the part of the composer or performer can be successful (in which case the musical piece reflects this intention) or unsuccessful (in which case the music seems expressive of something else, or of nothing at all). Second, whether the *listener* experiences an emotion as a response to a musical piece is also a separate issue from whether the piece itself expresses that emotion. As already mentioned, cases of mismatch between the expressive character of music and the aroused emotions are too common for these two notions to be considered equivalent. Third, expressiveness is not the same as the emotional character of music. Music can exhibit the character of a certain emotion (it can be adequately described with emotion terms) without necessarily being expressive. A musical piece may be adequately described as "sad" or "mournful" – as Kivy said that Telemann wrote "yards and yards of mournful music" – but still fail to be expressive.[315] Finally, as my own discussion of these conflicting views no doubt illustrates, the term "expressiveness" is unfortunately left somewhat vague by these theories. It seems that musical expressiveness does stand in some kind of relationship with each of the other phenomena it was equated with, but it is still not clear what the relationship is in any particular case, and what exactly musical expressiveness involves.

1.4 Emotivists vs. Cognitivists: Musically Induced Emotions

This is as much as to say that these theories have to be further refined before their adequacy can be properly assessed. Even without refinement, however, they can be brought into a relationship with many empirical findings of experimental psychology. For example, most of the philosophers writing about music and the emotions, probably prompted by their own experience and the widespread testimony of other people, generally assume the possibility of musically-evoked emotions.[316] It is an

---

[315] *Ibid.*

[316] Hanslick, *On the Musically Beautiful*, pp. 3-4. Also see Robinson, *Deeper than Reason.*

assumption implicit in their accounts, and indeed it is accepted much more widely, both within philosophy and outside it, both by musically cultivated people and by people who merely "like listening to music" without having any significant musical culture. Davies defends this generally accepted view by appealing to the fact that moods, but also expressive appearances can affect people, in the sense of being contagious: "If one wished to feel happy one might do so by surrounding oneself with happy-looking people."[317]

This view called "emotivism" was nevertheless disputed by some philosophers who argued that music does not evoke emotions, and that instead these emotions are only perceived in the music. Kivy is the most explicit opponent of the view, considering himself a "cognitivist" in this debate, and supported by some notable psychologists working on musical emotions.[318]

Kivy argues against the common belief that music arouses ordinary emotions. He holds instead that music can evoke the so-called "musical emotions", such as excitement, exhilaration, wonder, awe, or enthusiasm.[319] By these he means the emotional "high" one gets when experiencing something that is experienced as beautiful, wonderful, sublime, etc., and that is exactly the feeling that one gets when listening to great, wonderful, magnificent music. Kivy presents an object-belief-feeling analysis of how music moves us emotionally. According to his analysis of emotion in general, when an emotion is experienced, there is, in the ordinary, normal cases, an object of the emotion. For example, if we are angry, the person we are angry at is the object of anger. Furthermore, Kivy claims, ordinarily, people experience an emotional state for a reason, which can be cashed out in terms of a belief or set of beliefs: "I am angry at my friend because I believe he cheated me in a poker game".

---

[317] Davies, *Musical Meaning and Expression*, p. 304.

[318] Peter Kivy, *Introduction to a Philosophy of Music* (Oxford: Clarendon Press, 2002). Also see Peter Kivy, *Sound Sentiment: An Essay on the Musical Emotions, Including the Complete Text of The Corded Shell* (Philadelphia: Temple University Press, 1989), and Vladimir Konečni, "Does Music Induce Emotion? A Theoretical and Methodological Analysis," *Psychology of Aesthetics Creativity and the Arts* 2, no. 2 (2008): 115-129.

[319] Kivy, *Introduction to a Philosophy of Music*, p. 130-131.

Finally, in ordinary cases of emotive arousal, an emotion frequently has a feeling component. Emotions are usually said to be felt.[320] When this analysis is applied to music, Kivy continues, the "*object* of the emotion is (...) the beauty of the music; the *belief* is that the music is beautiful; the *feeling* is the kind of excitement or exhilaration or awe or wonder, etc. that such beauty customarily arouses."[321] If one responds to music's expressiveness, one responds with admiration or disappointment to the way in which this expressiveness is realized. A person may be moved to the point of tears by how well the music attains its expressive effects.[322] In Kivy's own words, "(...) what deeply moves me emotionally by music is just that very beauty, or magnificence, or other positive aesthetic properties it may possess to a very high degree. The object of the 'musical emotion,' if I may so call it, for want of a better term, is music. (What else?) Or, more exactly, the object of the musical emotion is the set of features in the music that the listener believes are beautiful, magnificent, or in some other ways aesthetically admirable to a high degree."[323] Kivy adds that many people are mistakenly convinced that they are made melancholy by melancholy music, fearful by fearful music, cheerful by cheerful music. What is happening to them is that, if the music is beautifully melancholy, or beautifully fearful, or beautifully cheerful, then this music moves them to a high state of emotional excitement with melancholy or fearfulness or cheerfulness as its object; and when this happens, they mistake this emotive excitement for melancholy in the first instance, fear in the second instance, cheerfulness in the third, since these are its objects.[324] He concludes by admitting that he has no proof or evidence that that is what is happening, but that it is not an unreasonable suggestion, and that "perhaps the psychologists can do something with it."[325] In the next section, we will see that experimental psychologists did do a lot of work on the possibility of musical induction of ordinary

---

[320] Kivy, *op.* cit., pp. 125-6.

[321] *Ibid.,* pp. 130-1.

[322] Kivy, *Sound Sentiment*, p. 231.

[323] Kivy, *Introduction to a Philosophy of Music*, p. 129.

[324] *Ibid.,* 133-4.

[325] *Ibid.*

emotions. Although the results are not completely conclusive, they seem to go against Kivy's position rather than support it.

Omission of Hanslick

Before proceeding to the section on the empirical work related to these debates, one thing should be noted. It might seem that the presentation of the main views on music and emotions omits one key name that is mentioned in almost every philosophical work on this topic, namely, Eduard Hanslick. However, even though Hanslick is indeed often appealed to in these debates, I consider his view mostly misrepresented in the contemporary literature.[326] Contrary to the widespread depictions of Hanslick as denying musical expressiveness, he never denied its existence, though he devoted no discussion to it, just as he did not deny the musical induction of emotions. He was mostly interested in highlighting the significance of specifically musical meaning and specifically musical beauty (see Chapter 1). His arguments against the "emotional aesthetics" are often mistakenly understood as denying that music expresses and arouses emotions – which Hanslick explicitly allows,[327] denying only that these emotional reactions constitute the purpose of music, and rejecting the possibility of unequivocally depicting emotions by music (as opposed to their loose and insufficiently determinate expression). Thus, Hanslick's theory on the relationship between music and the emotions focuses on aspects not relevant to the topics presented here, and that is why his views are not discussed in this chapter.

---

[326] For a detailed demonstration of this misrepresentation, see Srećković, *op. cit.*

[327] "[My] thesis first and foremost opposes the widespread view that music is supposed to 'represent feelings.' It is incomprehensible to me the way some people insist that this implies an absolute lack of feelings in music" – Hanslick, *On the Musically Beautiful*, Introduction, p. xxii. See also Hanslick *op.* cit., pp. 3-4.

2 Experiments Related to Emotions in Music

As already noted, most philosophers of music take for granted that music induces everyday emotions. Even though it seems self-evident to the majority of people that music does evoke genuine emotions, it is actually quite difficult to demonstrate that this belief is true, and that it is not merely a result of confusion on the part of the subjects. The experiments which will be presented show that the relationship between music and emotions, especially between musically expressed and aroused emotions is in fact more complex than it is represented in the philosophical literature.

2.1 Experiments Related to Musical Expressiveness

The first part of the chapter presented three philosophical theories of musical expressiveness: the expression theory which defines expressiveness as a consequence of the (actual or implied) composer's intentions and emotions; the arousal theory which holds that expressiveness is only attributed to music as a reflection of the feelings of the listeners aroused by the music; and the so-called 'appearance emotionalism' theory which explains the experience of music as expressive arises out of perceiving similarities between musical dynamics and human expressive behavior. All three theories define musical expressiveness by equating it with some other type of emotional experience related to music. While expressiveness may stand in some kind of relationship with each of the other phenomena it was equated with, all three attempts of definition face serious problems (which were explained above). Thus even though most listeners have an intuitive understanding of what expressiveness is in the experience of listening to music, the term itself is still left vague even after the philosophical analyses. This constitutes the crucial obstacle in exploring musical expressiveness empirically: the criteria for what musical expressiveness is are still unknown. In other words, even if we wished to test the correlations between expressiveness and any of the three *definientia*, it is not clear what exactly should be looked for as an empirical instance of musical expressiveness.

This section will instead focus on a brief analysis of the third theory of musical expressiveness. Davies' account on the emotional characteristics in appearances is most probably mistaken in its characterization of musical expressiveness, and rightly accused of conflating expressiveness with the emotional character of music. Nevertheless, by virtue of such conflation, his claims that the properties of music itself may carry emotional character are subject to empirical research.

Namely, in the philosophical literature dealing with musical expressiveness, expressiveness is usually related to meaning, almost always in an overly vague way which does not reveal much about the relationship between meaning and expressiveness. It was already mentioned that Davies' approach to expressiveness is in fact very similar to the 'expressionist' theories of musical meaning which claim that through the use of correspondences between musical elements and particular emotions, music can express emotional meaning (see Chapter 1, Section 1.1). Thus the same studies that are relevant for the theories of emotional meaning may be relevant for Davies' theory of expressiveness.

The experiment conducted by Koelsch and colleagues (presented in detail in Chapter 1, Section 2.3) provides results that are complementary to Davies' view. The participants of the Koelsch study were asked to rate the 'semantic fit' between particular musical excerpts and particular concepts, and their neurological reactions were recorded in order to affirm their subjective impressions. The experiment showed that the subjects without musical training who are presented with unfamiliar instrumental musical sequences similarly associate the sequences with particular concepts.[328] The list included a great number of both abstract and concrete concepts, among others: limitedness, wideness, needle, river, king, circle, glass, mischief, devotion, staircase, blossom, pearls, hero, celebration, leave, arrival, red, blue, etc. The experiment was successful in confirming its hypothesis of the semantic relationships, however, the exact mechanism underlying the perception of the 'semantic fit' between musical structure and particular concepts was not discussed in the study.

Two interesting implications can be derived from the connection between Davies' account and Koelsch's results. First, Davies' analysis may be useful in

---

[328] Koelsch et al., "Music, Language and Meaning: Brain Signatures of Semantic Processing."

explaining the underlying mechanisms of at least some of the semantic relations found in the experiment. The experimenters derived from their findings the conclusions solely regarding music: music can convey much more conceptual information than was previously supposed.[329] We can, however, widen the scope of this conclusion to concepts as well. Concepts themselves have many associations with the characteristics which can be described with words related to space, movement, or emotional character. Thus, to use Davies' terms, there may be an analogy in the manner in which we experience (emotional and other) characteristics related to particular concepts and the characteristics of their musical counterparts used in the study. This similarity in ways of experiencing them can explain the perceived semantic relationships between them. Thus it may not be surprising that Schoenberg's sequence containing a high pitched, harsh 'squeaking' (almost piercing) tone on the string was perceived as related to the word 'needle';[330] Bach's several parallelly meandering sequences of tones were associated with the word 'river';[331] Beethoven's texturally rich orchestral sequence lead by the wide and loud movements of the brass section was associated with 'hero';[332] Carl Nielsen's fast and bouncy (or playful) melody in the strings accompanied by a syncopated beat on timpani was associated with 'mischief'.[333] Thus we extended Davies' view formulated solely for the relationship between music and expressive human behavior to more general associations between musical features and concepts.

The second interesting implication follows from applying Koelsch's results to Davies' account of expressiveness. Davies limits the possibility of musical expression only to the emotions which have characteristic behavioral expressions, based on the

---

[329] Koelsch, *op. cit.*, p. 303.

[330] The sequence was taken from Arnold Schönberg, String Trio, Op 45.

[331] Taken from J. S. Bach, Das wohltemperierte Klavier (The Well-Tempered Clavier), BWV 846-869 Prelude in C minor.

[332] Taken from Ludwig van Beethoven, Egmont Overture, Op 84.

[333] Taken from Carl Nielsen, (1865-1931) Symphony No 2 "The Four Temperaments", Op.16 IV: Allegro sanguineo.

assumed inability of music to convey conceptual content.[334] Since only the expressive dynamics or movement is common to music and the emotions, music can resemble only the aspects of emotions which can manifested by human expressive behavior. Koelsch's study showed, however, that similarities or associations between music and the extra-musical world can be much broader, and that many phenomena or events other than expressive human behavior share the characteristics commonly found in music. Davies' account could thus be complemented by many other possibilities, or multiple paths and factors through which music achieves meaning or expression, be it emotional or conceptual.

In the following sections, I will present the empirical work related to the question of the arousal of emotions of music, far more extensive than the work done on the vague term such as 'expressiveness'.

2.2 Experiments Related to the Musical Arousal of Emotion

As already mentioned, most of the experimental studies on music focus on music's influence on people's emotions rather than on the expressiveness. This tendency is understandable, since it is primarily motivated by possible medical application of these results, and the search for the benefits of music therapy in treating neurological and other disorders.[335] Thus, the debate between the emotivists and the cognitivists will receive more attention in the empirical part of this chapter. The studies which will be presented in the following sections attempt either to demonstrate that full-blown everyday emotions can be evoked by music (thus supporting the emotivist view), or to show that the studies which purportedly succeed in this demonstration were methodologically unsound and therefore have questionable results (and thus try to refute evidence for emotivism and thus support the cognitivist view).

---

[334] Davies, *Musical Meaning and Expression*, pp. 225-6.

[335] Levitin and Tirovolas, "Current Advances in the Cognitive Neuroscience of Music," p. 211.

General Attitude Toward the Emotivist vs. Cognitivist Debate

The majority of the literature on musically evoked emotions favors the emotivist view. In a meta-analysis, Swaminathan and Schellenberg show that subjects belonging to various social groups consciously use music to regulate their emotional states – to relax, enhance mood, for motivation, etc.[336] Music is claimed to be particularly effective in moderating emotional states. Swaminathan and Schellenberg report findings of some studies which showed that after inducing a sad mood in the participants, listening to happy sounding music showed to be more powerful in improving mood than other manipulations. Self-selected "depressing" music was also shown to be more powerful than alternatives in changing a mood in the reverse direction.[337]

It is, however, sometimes questioned whether participants in these studies confuse felt emotions with the emotions they attribute to the music. The credibility of the subjective reports about the felt emotions was tested in studies which include physiological measures, and these studies confirm that listening to music often correlates with higher arousal (i.e. intensity, which is one of the two key dimensions of felt emotions), indicated by the increase in heart rate, respiratory rate, and electrodermal activity.[338] Experiencing emotions during listening to music has also been shown to be associated with patterns of activation of the amygdala, the hippocampus, and the hypothalamus.[339]

---

[336] Swathi Swaminathan and E. Glenn Schellenberg, "Current Emotion Research in Music Psychology," *Emotion Review* 7, no. 2 (2015), p. 191, referring to Lei Chen, Shuhua Zhou, and Jennings Bryant, "Temporal Changes in Mood Repair Through Music Consumption: Effects of Mood, Mood Salience, and Individual Differences," *Media Psychology* 9, (2007): 695-713.; Adam J. Lonsdale and Adrian C. North, "Why Do We Listen to Music? A Uses and Gratifications Analysis," *British Journal of Psychology* 102 (2011): 108-134.

[337] Merry J. Sleigh and Jordan McElroy, "The Effect of Music Listening Versus Written Reframing on Mood Management," *Music Perception* 31 (2014): 303-315.

[338] For more details about the arousal and valence dimension of emotion, see Chapter 1, Section 2.2.

[339] See Koelsch, "Brain Correlates of Music-Evoked Emotion."

Nevertheless, even the findings of the physiological indicators of the musically induced emotions raised serious, and in some aspects reasonable doubts. The most explicit opponent of the emotivist view, Vladimir Konečni, questions the validity of the empirical body of work used as a reference that music does induce genuine emotions. In the next section, I will present his main objections to the most popular studies which support the emotivist view.

2.3 Konečni's Criticism of the Popular Studies

Konečni claims that, contrary to the noticeable popularity, "among both music psychologists and the general public," of the emotivist view on musically induced emotions, the empirical literature which supports that view is unconvincing.[340]

His first criticism of this literature consists in claiming that there are not many studies which are in fact relevant for this issue, and that the mistaken belief that there exists a large body of empirical work is a result of confounding emotions and moods, which are to be distinguished by intensity, duration, suddenness-of-onset, and other known criteria.[341]

Further, he points out that there are serious methodological shortcomings even in some of the most cited and relevant studies. Perhaps most notably, musical *expression* of emotion has often been conflated with the *induction* of emotions by music.[342] This is not surprising since, as I have shown in the philosophical part of the chapter, expressiveness of music is not very well understood even by the philosophers of music, and additionally since many writers explicitly equate music's expressiveness of a particular emotions with the induction of that emotion in the listeners.

---

[340] Konečni, "Does Music Induce Emotion?", p. 115.

[341] *Ibid.*, pp. 115-16.

[342] *Ibid.*, p. 116.

An additional problem comes from the fact that even when the authors of empirical studies make a distinction between musical expression and induction of emotions, they themselves often continue to draw conclusions which seem to ignore the implications of the distinction.[343] In order to demonstrate this, Konečni reviews some of the key studies that are often cited as evidence of the fact that music does induce emotions, and analyzes the shortcomings in their methodology.

Misleading Titles of the Studies

Some of the major empirical studies on musical emotions, which do not even examine the induction of emotion, may be misleading through imprecise wording. Sometimes the researchers use formulations which suggest that the subjects of the studies experienced emotions, even when the induction of emotions was not at all a part of the experiment. Sometimes these misleading formulations are found in the very titles of articles.[344]

Unclear Instructions

In other cases, the confusion of musical expression and induction of emotions is found in the instructions given to the participants, such as: "Your next task is to adjust the slider continuously to indicate *the amount of emotion* at each point in time"[345] (italics added by Konečni). In cases such as this, it is unclear whether the participants were rating their own emotional states, the emotions perceived in the music, or a combination of both, or sometimes one and sometimes the other. Such imprecisions in

---

[343] *Ibid.*

[344] *Ibid.*, p. 118., referring to Patrik Juslin, "Cue Utilization in Communication of Emotion in Music Performance: Relating Performance to Perception," *Journal of Experimental Psychology: Human Perception and Performance* 26 (2000): 1797-1813.

[345] Konečni, *op. cit.*, p. 118., referring to Carol L. Krumhansl, "Topic in Music: An Empirical Study of Memorability, Openness, and Emotion in Mozart's String Quartet in C major and Beethoven's String Quartet in A minor," *Music Perception* 16 (1998), p. 126.

the instructions, he adds, "may have serious methodological and conceptual consequences."[346]

Unwarranted Conclusions

Konečni proceeds to present in more detail the methodological errors of several repeatedly cited studies which he believes had a significant role in misleading the scientific community into the belief that the musical induction of emotions is empirically demonstrated. One of such studies is Nykliček, Thayer, and van Doornen study titled "Cardiorespiratory differentiation of musically *induced emotions*"[347] (italics added by Konečni). This study reports on the cardio-respiratory data which allegedly shows that listening to different pieces of music gives rise to different emotions. However, their methodology suggests solely that the participants were differentially physiologically aroused by the given pieces of music. Nykliček and colleagues did not further elaborate on whether the physiological arousal of the participants resulted in them experiencing genuine emotions.[348] Further, the subjects were explicitly instructed to indicate on a rating scale "how strongly each emotion is *expressed* by the music"[349] (italics added by Konečni). Nykliček and colleagues only cited Thayer's (one of the authors of the study) doctoral dissertation in order to justify that the ratings of expressed and the induced emotions are "highly correlated", but they do not provide any data in their own paper.[350]

---

[346] Konečni, *op. cit.*, p. 118.

[347] Ivan Nykliček, Julian F. Thayer, Lorenz J. P. Van Doornen, "Cardiorespiratory differentiation of musically induced emotions," *Journal of Psychophysiology* 11, no. 4 (1997): 304-321.

[348] Konečni, *op. cit.*, p. 120.

[349] Nykliček et al., *op. cit.*, p. 307.

[350] *Ibid.*, p. 310. See also Julian F. Thayer, "Multiple Indicators Of Affective Response To Music" (PhD diss., New York University, 1986).

Another example of such methodologically flawed studies is Waterman's study, in which the subjects were instructed to "press the button when the music causes *something to happen to [them]*"[351] (italics added by Konečni). It is unclear what the subjects reported on, especially whether they reported on having an emotional experience. Further, Konečni believes that the physiological changes detected in the study (facial muscle activity, foot-tapping, increased heart rate) are not sufficient for the conclusion that the participants were experiencing a genuine emotional state.[352]

Predisposing the Participants

One of the most influential studies cited in support of the assumption of musically induced emotions is the famous 1997 study by Carol Krumhansl, in which the participants were asked to indicate the amount of a certain emotion (sadness, happiness, fear) they experienced while listening to particular pieces of music.[353] Even if at least some of the participants were actually rating their emotional states and not the music, Konečni objects, before listening, the subjects read the following instructions: "Music is thought to have many effects on people, including influencing their emotions. Indicate how much fear you are experiencing from moment to moment by moving the slider from left to right. The slider should be at the far left if you feel none of that emotion, and at the far right if you feel that emotion as strongly as you have in response *to music* in the past" (italics added by Konečni).[354] These instructions involve two claims. They proclaim that music influences emotions, and

---

[351] Mitch Waterman, "Emotional Responses to Music: Implicit and Explicit Effects in Listeners and Performers," *Psychology of Music* 24, no. 1 (1996), p. 56.

[352] Konečni, *op. cit.*, p. 120.

[353] Krumhansl, "An Exploratory Study of Musical Emotions and Psychophysiology."

[354] Konečni, *op. cit.*, p. 121.

they limit the emotional experience of the subjects to the musical domain.[355] Thus the participants may have been more prone to report on feeling emotions than if they had not been predisposed to do so by the instructions.[356]

Failure at Replicating the Results

In order to test the interference of the instruction wording with the participants' self-reports, Krumhansl's results were tested in subsequent studies with two versions of alternate instructions. In this replication study, the participants listened to the "sad" pieces from Krumhansl's original study (Albinoni's Adagio in G minor for Strings and Barber's Adagio for Strings), and were asked to rate them on the "sad" scale (0 = Not at all; 8 = Very much). One group of subjects received the same instructions which were used in the original study: "Music is thought to have many effects on people, including influencing their emotions (...).". The other group received the altered instructions which started with: "Researchers disagree on whether or not music has an effect on emotion (...)." The results showed that the difference in the instructions had significant effects. The original instructions gave rise to the 5.70 sadness rating for Barber and 5.03 for Albinoni, and the alternate, "Researchers disagree..." instructions resulted in lower sadness ratings, namely, 3.32 and 4.25.[357]

In another variation, when the Krumhansl instruction "Using the following scale, rate how YOU FELT while listening to the music selection" was replaced by "Using the adjectives below, describe THE MUSIC selection you just heard" (capital letters in the original text), the "sadness" ratings for Barber and Albinoni rose significantly to 6.12 and 6.87. In other words, ratings of the music's expressiveness were significantly higher than the ratings of the participants' own emotional state.[358]

---

[355] Konečni adds that in fairness to Krumhansl, the title of her paper contains the words "musical emotions," but this limitation is partially lost both within the article and when the article is generally cited – Konečni, *op. cit.*, p. 121.

[356] *Ibid.*, p. 120.

[357] *Ibid.*, p. 121.

[358] *Ibid.*, p. 121.

This shows how slight differences in formulating the instructions, perhaps a result of the author's unspoken theoretical assumptions, may influence the results of the study. Subsequently, Konečni adds, Krumhansl herself compared the physiological results she gathered to the results gathered in other major studies of the physiology of emotions, finding "little correspondence with [her] results".[359]

Konečni takes the lack of correspondence between these groups of results to suggest that Krumhansl's study cannot be unequivocally accepted as supporting the assumption that music induces emotions. His criticism rightly directs us toward a more cautious approach to even the most often cited studies in this field. The empirical body of work supporting emotivism indeed should be reexamined. Konečni's criticism provides an important methodological lesson for the philosophers who would wish to adopt the conclusions of experimental psychology without getting familiar with its methods.

2.4 A More Cautious Study on the Aroused Emotions

Perhaps by virtue of criticisms such as this, the authors of the following studies were more thorough in designing their experiments, and have thus provided us with more convincing results. In this section, I will present in detail the study which has reportedly demonstrated that music does induce genuine emotions, in order to expose the eventual methodological errors, or lack thereof. I will subsequently show that the methodological soundness of the study is further supported by the fact that it was subsequently replicated by another group of researchers (also to be presented below).

Lundqvist and colleagues wanted to investigate whether music with different emotional expressions (happy and sad) evokes different emotional responses in the listeners. They recorded subjective self-reports of the participants as well as the

---

[359] *Ibid.*, referring to Krumhansl "An Exploratory Study of Musical Emotions and Psychophysiology," p. 349.

physiological reactions commonly associated with particular emotions.[360] They focused on happiness and sadness based on the previous findings that these two emotions are easily expressed in music,[361] and that they seem to be common responses to music.[362] It should also be noted that the authors of the study did not indicate whether they believed that music is *expressive* of these emotions, or merely adequately described by the emotion related words (which would fit Davies' definition of expressiveness).

Measuring Felt Emotions

First Step: Defining Emotions

The measures recorded in the experiment were chosen based on the definition of emotion the authors of the study have already adopted. Lundqvist and colleagues acknowledge the lack of consensus on a precise definition of emotions, and settle on basing their approach on the agreement that exists among many researchers that "emotional responses are manifested in three components: experience, expression, and physiology."[363] The adopt the view that "emotions give rise to affective

---

[360] Lars-Olov Lundqvist et al., "Emotional Responses to Music: Experience, Expression, and Physiology," *Psychology of Music* 37, no. 1 (2009): 61-90.

[361] Patrik Juslin and Petri Laukka, "Communication of Emotions in Vocal Expression and Music Performance: Different Channels, Same Code?" *Psychological Bulletin* 129, no. 5 (2003): 770-814.

[362] Patrik Juslin, and Petri Laukka, "Expression, Perception, and Induction of Musical Emotions: A Review and a Questionnaire Study of Everyday Listening," *Journal of New Music Research* 33, no. 3 (2004): 217-238.

[363] Lundqvist et al., *loc. cit.*, referring to Ross Buck, "Social and Emotional Functions in Facial Expression and Communication: The Read-Out Hypothesis," *Biological Psychology* 38, no. 2-3 (1994): 95-115.; Paul Ekman, "Facial Expression and Emotion," *American Psychologist* 48, no. 4 (1993): 384-392.; Carroll E. Izard, *Human emotions* (New York: Plenum, 1977).; Robert W. Levenson, "Human Emotion: A Functional View," in *The Nature of Emotion: Fundamental Questions*, ed. Paul Ekman and Richard J. Davidson (New York:

experiences such as feelings of happiness, sadness, pleasure, and displeasure; activate widespread *physiological* adjustments to the evoking conditions; and lead to *expressive* behaviors. Lundqvist and colleagues elaborate shortly on how these three components can be investigated experimentally, and how the results help decide whether music does induce emotions" (italics in the original).[364] The following sub-sections will present an elaboration of how these three components were measured in the study, and how we can know whether the results are relevant for the emotivist versus cognitivist debate.

First Component: Subjective Experience

Subjective experience, or feeling, has a long tradition of being considered the essential element of emotion. Lundqvist and colleagues add that its importance lies in integrating all other components and being the basis of the conscious representation and regulation of emotion.[365] Subjective emotional experience is most commonly measured through self-reports, which can be differently designed: as phenomenological descriptions, rating scales, or multiple-choice formats.[366]

Lundqvist and colleagues chose self-reports based on rating scales, and applied them to lists of emotion related adjectives. This technique was used in earlier research in which participants differentiated experienced emotions evoked by various types of stimuli such as imagery, film segments, or facial expressions, and also

---

Oxford University Press, 1994), 123-126.; Howard Leventhal, "A Perceptual-Motor Theory of Emotion," *Information (International Social Science Council)* 21, no. 6 (1982): 819-845.

[364] Lundqvist et al., *op. cit.*, p. 61-2.

[365] Lundqvist et al., *op. cit.*, p. 62., referring to Klaus R. Scherer, "Why Music does not Produce Basic Emotions: Pleading for a New Approach to Measuring the Emotional Effects of Music," in *Proceedings of the Stockholm Music Acoustics Conference*, ed. Roberto Bresin (Stockholm, Sweden: Royal Institute of Technology, 2003), 25-28.

[366] Lundqvist et al., *op. cit.*, p. 62.

music.[367] In this study, the aim was to measure the participants' experience of happiness, sadness, surprise, anger, interest, fear, and disgust induced by the musical stimuli.

Each of these emotions was represented by three adjectives on the list. Sadness was represented by 'sad', 'downhearted', and 'blue'; happiness was represented by 'happy', 'amused', and 'joyful'; anger by 'angry', 'mad', and 'irritated', etc.[368] For each of the adjectives on the list, the subjects had to indicate the degree of intensity on a scale ranging from "not at all", "slightly", "moderately", "rather strong", to "very strong". The scores of the three adjectives which describe the same emotion were added up.[369]

Lundqvist and colleagues acknowledge various methodological problems with self-reports mentioned by Konečni. They note that the difficulty of the listeners to differentiate between their own emotions and the ones perceived in music might be alleviated with use of the clear and precise instructions which specify whether the subjects should direct their attention to their own emotional states or the qualities of music.[370] They also mention another problem, of the subjects answering what they believe the researchers expect of them, or what seems to be the most acceptable answer. To deal with this, they propose the technique of 'cover stories' which distract the subjects from the hypotheses being tested in the experiment.[371] They used this technique in their own study.

---

[367] *Ibid.*, p. 62. Also see Patrik Juslin and John Sloboda, *Music and Emotion: Theory and Research* (New York: Oxford University Press, 2001).

[368] Lundqvist et al., *op. cit.*, p. 65.

[369] *Ibid.*

[370] *Ibid.*, p. 62.

[371] *Ibid.*

Second Component: Physiological Expression of Emotions

The subjective feeling is usually accompanied by the appropriate expression of emotion. Since the face has an important role in the expression of emotions, and there are particular facial muscles which are responsible for different facial expressions, Lundqvist and colleagues tested the correlations between the activity of these muscles and different emotional characteristics of music presented to the subjects. They based their method on findings of the previous research, which showed that activity in the regions of *zygomaticus major* (muscles used when smiling) and *corrugator supercilii* (muscles used when frowning) is related to the degree of valence (pleasantness or unpleasantness) of emotionally laden imagery,[372] facial expressions,[373] vocal expressions,[374] and auditory stimuli in general.[375] In studies which focused on music, the results were consistent with the these findings: they showed increased *zygomatic* (smiling) activity in response to music with positive valence, and increased *corrugator* (frowning) activity in response to music with negative valence.[376]

---

[372] Alan Fridlund, Gary Schwartz, and Stephen Fowler, "Pattern Recognition of Self-Reported Emotional State From Multiple-Site Facial EMG Activity During Affective Imagery," *Psychophysiology* 21, no. 6 (1984): 622-637. Also see Gary E. Schwartz et al., "Facial Muscle Patterning to Affective Imagery in Depressed and Nondepressed Subjects," *Science* 192, no. 4238 (1976): 489-491.

[373] Ulf Dimberg, "Facial Reactions to Facial Expressions," *Psychophysiology* 19, no.6 (1982): 643-647. See also Lars-Olov Lundqvist, "Facial EMG Reactions to Facial Expressions: A Case of Facial Emotional Contagion?" *Scandinavian Journal of Psychology* 36(2), (1995): 130-141.; and Lars-Olov Lundqvist and Ulf Dimberg, "Facial Expressions Are Contagious," *Journal of Psychophysiology* 9, no. 2 (1995): 203-211.

[374] Jari K. Hietanen, Viekko Surakka, and Ilkka Linnankoski, "Facial Electromyographic Responses to Vocal Affect Expressions," *Psychophysiology* 35, no. 5 (1998): 530-536.

[375] Margaret M. Bradley and Peter J. Lang, "Affective Reactions to Acoustic Stimuli," *Psychophysiology* 37, no. 2 (2000): 204-215. Also see Lutz Jäncke et al., "Facial EMG Responses to Auditory Stimuli," *International Journal of Psychophysiology* 22, no 1-2 (1996): 85-96.

[376] Lundqvist et al., *op. cit.*, p. 62., referring to Charlotte van Oyen Witvliet and Scott R. Vrana, "The Emotional Impact of Instrumental Music on Affect Ratings, Facial EMG,

Lundqvist and colleagues thus included the electromyographic (EMG) measurements over the facial muscle regions which they will compare with the emotional qualities of the music presented to the participants.[377]

Third Component: Autonomic Responses

In regard to the third component, while the responses of the autonomic nervous system (ANS) are known to accompany experiences of emotions, it is still a controversial issue to what extent different emotions require *different* patterns of the ANS activity.[378] Based on the view that emotions should result in the subject adjusting to the (different) evoking conditions in the environment, Lundqvist and colleagues agree with other researchers[379] who have argued that at least some emotions *should* reflect specific autonomic activity, even though it is not certain whether it is indeed so. They cite previous studies on autonomic responses to other types of stimuli, such as imagery, film excerpts, or facial expressions, in which the autonomic changes seemed to differentiate among emotions, but add that these studies report merely on a relatively few cases.[380]

Autonomic Measures, and the Startle Reflex: Effects of Valence and Arousal," *Psychophysiology Supplement* 91 (1996).

[377] *Ibid.*, referring to John T. Cacioppo et al., "Electromyographic Activity Over Facial Muscle Regions Can Differentiate the Valence and Intensity of Affective Reactions," *Journal of Personality and Social Psychology* 50, no. 2 (1986): 260-268.

[378] Lundqvist et al., *op. cit.*, p. 62.

[379] Paul Ekman, Robert W. Levenson, and Wallace V. Friesen, "Autonomic Nervous System Activity Distinguishes Among Emotions," *Science* 221, no. 4616 (1983): 1208-1210. Also see Robert W. Levenson, Paul Ekman, and Wallace V. Friesen, "Voluntary Facial Action Generates Emotion-Specific Autonomic Nervous System Activity," *Psychophysiology* 27, no. 4 (1990): 363-384.

[380] Lundqvist et al., *op. cit.*, p. 63., referring to John T. Cacioppo, David J. Klein, Gary G. Berntson, and Elaine Hatfield, "The Psychophysiology of Emotion," in *Handbook of*

149

In regard to the studies which measured the autonomic activity while listening to *music*, most of them examined arousal (intensity) rather than valence (pleasantness/unpleasantness) dimension of an emotional response.[381] In a meta-study in which more than 130 studies were reviewed, it was shown that different musical features correlate with different arousal levels. Music with fast tempo, loud dynamics, and prominent rhythm, evokes an increase in muscle tension and heart rate. Music characterized as melodic, with slow tempo, soft dynamics, and legato style evokes a decrease in the same measures, and also in electrodermal activity.[382]

In regard to the valence dimension of emotion, however, Lundqvist and colleagues admit that only there is not much research on musically induced emotions which focused on valence. As a source of evidence that happy and fearful music induces higher heart rate than sad music Lundqvist and colleagues cite Krumhansl[383] and Nyklíček[384] – the same two studies that Konečni criticized for methodological inadequacies (see Section 2.3). Nevertheless, Lundqvist and colleagues hypothesize a correlation between positive valence and higher skin conductance and temperature, as well as a correlation between negative valence and lower skin conductance and temperature,[385] and they test these correlations in their own study (which will be presented below).

Emotion, ed. Michael Lewis and Jeannette M. Haviland (New York: Guilford Press, 1993), 119-142.

[381] The valence and arousal dimension of emotion are discussed in more detail in Chapter 1, Section 2.2.

[382] Dale L. Bartlett, "Physiological Responses to Music and Sound Stimuli," in *Handbook of Music Psychology*, ed. Donald A. Hodges (San Antonio, TX: Institute for Music Research Press, 1996), 343-385.

[383] Krumhansl, "An Exploratory Study of Musical Emotions and Psychophysiology."

[384] Nyklíček et al., "Cardiorespiratory differentiation of musically induced emotions."

[385] Lundqvist et al., *op. cit.*, p. 63.

An Additional Indicator: Coherence of the Responses

On top of these three components of emotions, response coherence, or 'response synchronization' is considered to be an important characteristic of emotions. Response coherence means that there is a corresponding response in all three mentioned components during an emotional experience. However, not many studies have actually demonstrated coherence among the responses belonging to each component,[386] and whether such coherence exists is still debated. It has been argued that the correspondence between the three components is not necessary for emotions and that absence of one component is not sufficient grounds to conclude the absence of an emotion. There are many examples of mismatch between the components, such as experiencing an emotion without showing a facial expression, or without the occurrence of some of the physiological changes, and it may depend on the situation or on the individual characteristics of the subject whether the responses belonging to each component will match.[387]

Nevertheless, taking these difficulties into account, if several measures of each component are used, and if the results show coherence among them, the credibility of the conclusion that an emotion occurred would clearly increase. In studies on music listening, evidence of coherence of the components would provide strong support to the view that music can evoke genuine emotions in the listeners. This would confirm the emotivist view on musically induced emotions. The cognitivist view that listeners merely perceive an emotion in music implies absence of autonomic and expressive responses (although it may allow for the misattributed subjective experience). This means that only emotivism predicts coherence of the components, while cognitivism predicts the absence of it.[388]

---

[386] One such study is Iris B. Mauss et al., "The Tie That Binds? Coherence Among Emotion Experience, Behavior, and Physiology," *Emotion* 5, no. 2 (2005): 175-190.

[387] Lundqvist et al., *op. cit.*, p. 63., referring to Paul Ekman, "Universal and Cultural Differences in Facial Expressions of Emotions," in *Nebraska Symposium on Motivation* 1971, ed. James K. Cole (Lincoln, NE: University of Nebraska Press, 1972), 207-283.

[388] Lundqvist et al., *loc. cit.*

Procedure

The aim of the study is to examine the changes in the subjective, expressive, and autonomic reactions of the listeners, and additionally the coherence between these reactions. Lundqvist and colleagues formulated the hypotheses which will be tested on the basis of the definition of emotion presented above. The hypotheses state that when listening to happy and sad music, in comparison with sad music, happy music should lead to:

1. higher ratings of happiness;

2. lower ratings of sadness;

3. no change in ratings between fear, anger, disgust, or surprise;

4. higher *zygomatic* (smiling) muscle activity;

5. lower *corrugator* (frowning) muscle activity;

6. higher heart rate;

7. higher skin conductance;

8. higher finger temperature.

In order to additionally support the hypotheses, the results should show the overall coherence in the pattern of responses.[389]

The participants were 32 musically untrained university students. As stimuli, the researchers used simple songs in pop genre, one with a happy emotional expression, and the other with a sad expression. The songs were composed for the study to avoid interference of personal associations with the songs. The happy song was composed in major mode, with fast tempo and loud dynamics, and the sad song was in minor mode, with slow tempo and low dynamics.[390] The choice of the characteristic musical features of happy and sad music was based on the associations established in previous research on emotional expression in music.[391] In addition, the researchers tested the adequacy of the stimuli before the experiment by having a different group of students rate the emotions expressed in the songs.[392]

---

[389] *Ibid.*, p. 64.

[390] *Ibid.*

[391] See Juslin and Laukka, "Expression, Perception, and Induction of Musical Emotions."

[392] Lundqvist et al., *op. cit.*, p. 65.

The subjects were not informed about the purpose of the study. They were told that the study tested physiological reactions to music. In order to divert them from their facial muscles, they were told that the electrodes of the EMG measure sweat gland activity. They also received a cover story for the questionnaire on their subjective emotional experience, namely, that it was necessary to measure their tiredness and mood as a part of a control procedure.[393] They completed the questionnaire before hearing the songs, and then after each hearing of the song. There were two versions of the happy song and two versions of the sad song. Thus the participants gave self-reports five times in total. Their physiological reactions were measured during the whole procedure.[394]

As a precaution, the subjects were interviewed after the experiment about the experimental instructions. All of them reported being unaware of the real purpose of the experiment, and of the questionnaire and the facial EMG measurement.[395]

Results

1. Self-reports (subjective experience)

The results of the self-reports showed higher happiness ratings after listening to the happy songs, and higher sadness ratings after the sad songs, and the ratings of other emotions did not differ after either happy or sad songs.[396] This confirms Hypotheses 1-3 which concern the subjective component of emotions.

---

[393] *Ibid.*, p. 66.

[394] Lundqvist et al., *op. cit.*, pp. 64-5.

[395] *Ibid.*, pp. 65-6.

[396] *Ibid.*, p. 66.

2. Facial muscle measures (expression of emotions)

The overall results for the facial EMG measurement showed higher smiling muscle activity for happy than for sad music. This suggests that the smiling muscle activity is sensitive to the *valence* of the presented emotional stimuli.[397] The frowning muscle activity, however, did not change for different songs. Certain short-term changes in this muscle activity were observed, but insufficient for supporting the respective hypothesis.[398] Thus, Hypothesis 4 was confirmed, while Hypothesis 5 was refuted.

3. Heart rate, skin conductance, and finger temperature (autonomic responses)

The results for ANS activity (involving skin conductance, finger temperature, and heart rate) revealed less straightforward results. Only for the skin conductance measure, the results were as predicted: happy music evoked a significant increase in skin conductance levels than sad music, confirming Hypothesis 7.

The results for the finger temperature were, however, contrary to the predictions. Instead of inducing higher finger temperature than sad music, it seems that happy music induced lower temperature. Lundqvist and colleagues attempt to explain this lack of correlation by claiming that the previous studies on finger temperature might be mistaken in inferring the correlation of finger temperature with valence, instead of arousal dimension of emotional response to music.[399] In regard to the experimental hypothesis, this would mean that even though the specific correlation postulated in this study (between valence and finger temperature) was refuted by the results, the more general assumption that there are specific autonomic responses for different emotions may still be accurate (e.g. finger temperature may be an indicator of the arousal dimension of emotions). Nevertheless, for now the results do not seem to support Hypothesis 8.

---

[397] *Ibid.*, pp. 66-7.

[398] *Ibid.*

[399] *Ibid.*, p. 68.

The results of the heart rate measurements also did not show significant differences for different songs. The prediction concerning the increase of heart rate was, thus not fulfilled.[400] Thus, Hypothesis 6 was refuted.

Conclusion of the Study

To summarize, happy music, compared to sad music, leads to higher happiness ratings (Hypothesis 1), lower sadness ratings (Hypothesis 2), and no significant differences in ratings of other emotions (Hypothesis 3). Further, happy music seemed to induce higher smiling muscle activity (Hypothesis 4), and higher skin conductance levels (Hypothesis 7). On the other hand, the results did not show the existence of the predicted correlations for the frowning muscle activity (Hypothesis 5), heart rate (Hypothesis 6), and finger temperature (Hypothesis 8).

In regard to the three components of emotions, the results can be described in the following way. The responses related to the subjective experience (measured by the self-report ratings), occurred in full as hypothesized by Hypotheses 1-3, supporting all three hypotheses concerning the first component. The responses related to the expression of emotions occurred partly: only the smiling muscle activities changed as predicted by Hypotheses 4 and 5, while the frowning muscle activity did not behave as predicted, thus supporting only one of two hypotheses concerning the second component. The responses related to the autonomic activity showed the least agreement with the predictions, since only skin conductance levels showed significant changes, while finger temperature and heart rate did not change as predicted, thus supporting only one of three hypotheses concerning the third component. Finally, in regard to the coherence between these three components, we can conclude that the results show a certain degree of coherence – since the significant changes did occur in all three components of emotions. However, not all predicted correlations were established in the study.

---

[400] *Ibid.*

Lundqvist and colleagues offer possible explanations that attribute the lack of correlations to the external factors. Perhaps there were shortcomings of the music composed for the experiment, and perhaps the correlation with temperature was displaced, and should be sought with another dimension of emotion (arousal) than the one hypothesized (valence).[401] Whether we find these explanations convincing or not, Lundqvist and colleagues believe that, even though not all of the hypotheses were confirmed, the results show a sufficient degree of coherence between the responses belonging to different components to indicate the existence of a genuine emotional response to music, which can be taken to support the emotivist position.

A Replication Study

In 2018, Bullack and colleagues attempted to replicate and extend the findings of the Lundqvist experiment.[402] They assumed that similar patterns of responses would occur in behavioral as well as physiological measures. The procedure was also similar to the Lundqvist study, except for the slight changes. Namely, the Bullack study used instrumental film music instead of vocal music, and added one additional parameter – the respiratory rate, because previous research has shown that emotional reactions are frequently accompanied by changes in the respiratory system as well.[403] Their results showed that respiratory rate (a measure not included in the Lundqvist study) increased in response to happy music only, but not in the presence of sad music. In other words, the participants responded to happy music with relatively faster breathing as compared to sad music, while in the sad music condition, breathing was unaffected. This additional measure supports the existence of a higher arousal for happy music.[404]

---

[401] *Ibid.*, p. 68.

[402] Antje Bullack et al., "Psychophysiological Responses to 'Happy' and 'Sad' Music: A Replication Study," *Music Perception: An Interdisciplinary Journal* 35 no. 4 (2018): 502-517.

[403] *Ibid.*, pp. 503-4.

[404] *Ibid.*, pp. 509-511.

This supports the view that different emotional characteristics of music induce different autonomic responses in the listeners.

Apart from the additionally introduced respiratory rate measure, the measurements from the Lundqvist study were successfully replicated. A favorable exception was the measurement of the activity of the facial muscles, which showed even more support to the existence of different responses to different emotional characteristics of music than the Lundqvist results. Namely, while the EMG measurements also showed a greater *zygomaticus* region activity when listening to happy in comparison to the sad music, there was also an increase in *corrugator* activity when listening to sad music, which was not found in the Lundqvist study.[405] These patterns of changes in facial muscle activity thus lend even more support to the hypothesis of differential activation of these muscles in response to different emotional characteristics of music.

The results of the Lundqvist study and Bullack's replication study alleviate some of the worries brought about by Konečni's objections. By using clear instructions and cover stories, the methodology behind collecting subjective reports seems sufficiently sound to provide a certain level of assurance concerning the self-reports. The physiological results, on the other hand, do not completely support the hypothesis tested by Lundqvist and Bullack, that music induces differential autonomic emotional responses. Nevertheless, their hypothesis is more ambitious than the one relevant for the emotivism versus cognitivism debate. The evidence provided by their studies still suggests that emotions were induced by music, even if these emotions do not differ in autonomic activity. Further, the difficulty of demonstrating differential autonomic responses is not specifically related to the emotions evoked by *music*, but is instead a problem for general experimental research on emotions. If the lack of differential autonomic responses is relevant for the issue whether different emotions can be induced, it is relevant for induction by any kind of stimuli, and not only music.

In summary, even if the evidence provided by these studies does not support the differential responses hypothesis, it does seem to support the induction of genuine emotions in music listeners. The meta-study presented in the following section

---

[405] *Ibid.*, pp. 510-11.

provides further support for musical induction of emotions, but also for the differential responses hypothesis.

2.5 Koelsch's Complementary Analysis

The Lundqvist findings were further supported and complemented by the neurological research on musically induced emotions. The newest neurological research made rapid progress concerning the neural correlates of emotions in general.[406] Stefan Koelsch reviews the empirical literature relevant for musically induced emotions and summarizes their findings in a meta-study. Based on these findings, Koelsch concludes that the reactions associated with emotions in general can be induced by music as well. These reactions include changes in subjective feeling, autonomic and endocrine activity, and motoric reactions (such as facial expressions).[407] The neurological aspect of these studies is especially significant for the topic of this chapter, as additional evidence to the Lundqvist and Bullack findings on the physiological changes in skin conductance, temperature, and heart and respiration rate. The neurological findings show that music is able to induce activity changes in the regions of the brain which are associated with emotional experience. In the following sections, I will briefly present some of the most relevant conclusions of Koelsch's review which focus on the role of amygdala and hippocampus in musically induced emotions, complemented by the additional evidence from the studies on brain lesions and degenerative diseases.

Amygdala

The research on emotions in general found that the amygdala is involved in modulation and regulation of the emotions, in particular, in initiation, maintenance, and termination of emotions. The amygdala also has a role in the integration of

---

[406] Koelsch, "Brain Correlates of Music-Evoked Emotions," p. 170.

[407] *Ibid.*

emotional and cognitive information. The neurological research on musically induced emotions provides evidence that the amygdala is sensitive to the differences in joyful and fearful music.[408]

Hippocampus

The hippocampus is also known to have an important role in emotional reactions in general. In regard to the emotional responses to music, some studies show that there are changes in the activity of the hippocampus related to musically induced emotions such as joy, peacefulness, sadness, thrills, and tenderness.[409] In addition, there are studies which show that subjects with a reduced hippocampal volume have a lower tendency to experience tender positive emotions in general, and also show lower hippocampal activity in response to musical stimuli as well.[410]

Additional Neurophysiological Findings

Evidence collected from studies conducted with patients with degenerative diseases or brain lesions show that these subjects have impaired recognition of musically expressed emotions such as sadness, happiness, fear, or anger.[411] In other words, brain regions associated with experiencing emotions in general seem to also be responsible for recognizing emotions in *music*. This indicates that *experiencing* emotions might also be involved in perceiving emotions in music, or even that recognizing emotions in music perhaps depends on the ability to experience emotions.

In summary, a growing number of studies show that music can trigger changes in the neural structures which underlie emotions in general. Moreover, damaging of

---

[408] *Ibid.*, p. 172.

[409] *Ibid.*, p. 173.

[410] *Ibid.*, p. 174.

[411] *Ibid.*

these structures causes problems with recognition of emotions in music, and weaker (or none) emotional reactions to music.

These results, together with the results of the Lundqvist and Bullack study indicate that music can induce genuine emotions, and not merely subjective feelings. When the findings of all these studies are combined, they provide support to the emotivist view on musically induced emotions.

Conclusion of the Third Chapter

Asymmetry Between Expressiveness and Arousal

As we have seen, the writings on the relationship between music and the emotions focus mostly on two topics, namely, musical expressiveness and musical arousal of emotions. The reader probably noticed the asymmetry in the amount of attention dedicated to these topics between philosophical and experimental discussion of these topics. While philosophers wrote much more extensively on the expressiveness of music, probably finding it philosophically more interesting than the possibility of musical induction of emotions which they mostly took for granted, experimental psychologists put far greater effort in exploring musically induced emotions, almost certainly because of their significance for medical treatment.

Problems with Musical Expressiveness

Thus the philosophical discussions about expressiveness offer various accounts that attempt to define expressiveness by equating it with some other kinds of emotional experiences related to music, such as expressing emotions in the creation of a musical work, or experiencing emotions while listening to music, or finally perceiving emotions in music. None of the accounts of musical expressiveness I have considered is without serious shortcomings, and it is not clear how these shortcomings could be eliminated to arrive at a plausible account of musical expressiveness. The term in question is still left unhelpfully vague, even though most listeners have an intuitive understanding of what expressiveness is in the experience of listening to music. It is also possible that "musical expressiveness" is an inherently vague concept, and is in fact used to refer to different phenomena by different listeners. The phenomenon itself might lack an essential feature by which it could be pinned down. This would explain why it is so difficult for the contemporary philosophers of music to reduce it to one of the numerous components of the complex emotional experience of music listening.

Extending the Possibilities of Extra-Musical Character of Music

Vagueness of the concept of expressiveness can also explain why not much research, if at all, is dedicated to exploring expressiveness. Necessary and sufficient conditions for music's possessing the property of expressiveness are not familiar, and it is unclear how it can be a part of the empirical research. I proposed that Davies' account, which treats expressiveness as a kind of meaning, can be related to Koelsch's semantic priming study which shows that music shares characteristics with many phenomena or events other than expressive human behavior. Thus, Davies' account which limits the possibility of musical expression only to the emotions with characteristic behavioral expressions can be complemented with Koelsch's results which show that music can have much broader extra-musical characteristics, and associate listeners not only with emotional, but also with conceptual content.

Even though such conclusion may not be too helpful in rendering the concept of musical expressiveness more precise, it exposes the philosophical accounts as limited in focusing solely on one – emotional – aspect of expressiveness. It may thus be useful for the philosophers as a suggestion to consider the relationship between music and emotions not in isolation, but as a part of a broader network of associations between music and the extra-musical world.

Emotivist versus Cognitivist Debate

The debate on the possibility of musical arousal of emotions, on the other hand, is considerably more often referenced in the empirical studies, many of which explicitly attempt to resolve the debate. The results seem to fit the intuitions of the great majority of the philosophers of music. This experimental body of work provides strong evidence that music does induce genuine emotions. This evidence goes far beyond the impressions or subjective feelings of the listeners, and includes several physiological components generally associated with particular emotions as well.

The persisting disagreements concerning this issue could be explained by the fact that different authors define emotions differently, which results in their accepting or, alternatively, rejecting the same complex of phenomena as a genuine emotion. While some authors (such as Koelsch and Lundqvist) take the combination of a subjective feeling and definite physiological indicators to be sufficient for an emotional experience, others (such as Konečni and Kivy) take a definite cognitive aspect (defined in various ways) as highly significant for an experience to be considered a genuine emotion. Thus, the proponents of the former type of definition of emotions accept the emotivist view more easily than those who favor the latter type of definition. The resolution of this issue depends to a large extent on the debates in the general psychology of emotions and is made more difficult by the lack of consensus concerning the definition of emotions.

Interdisciplinary Lessons

The aim of this dissertation was examining the possible applicability of experimental results in philosophy of music. There are, however, insights that psychologists can acquire from the philosophical analyses as well. Just as Koelsch's results broaden the scope of possibilities of musical expressiveness and meaning, Davies' analysis may in turn complement Koelsch's results with an explanation of the underlying mechanisms of some of the semantic relations found in the experiment, by appealing to an analogy in the way of experiencing characteristics related to particular concepts and the characteristics of musical structure (see Section 2.1).

Suggestions for Further Research

With regard to suggestions for further research, it would be interesting to compare the results concerning musical emotions with the issue of musical meaning or the issue of assigning aesthetic value to musical compositions. Further research could test whether there are correlations between the emotions aroused by the music and value attributed to it. The correlations between the kind of meaning (emotional, formalistic, etc.) and the degree of emotional arousal in the listeners could also provide interesting insights. This will need to be addressed in another work.

Conclusion

The focus of this dissertation was the relationship between two seemingly distant fields: philosophical aesthetics of music on one side, and experimental psychology and cognitive neuroscience on the other side. The aim was determining the relationship between problems, conceptual frameworks, and domains of these two fields of inquiry. I attempted to answer the question whether the results of the empirical research contribute to philosophical aesthetics of music, in particular, whether some of the results and conclusions of the empirical research can be used as *arguments* in the debates in philosophy of music.

The motivation behind this project was mostly methodological. I was interested in learning whether a connection could be forged between abstract and normative problems of musical aesthetics on one side, and concrete and descriptive results of the experimental research on the other side. In order to forge this connection, I conducted a dispositionalist analysis of the concepts involved in aesthetic theories, such as value, meaning, form and content, and found their empirical counterparts involved in the experimental research: preference, pleasure, syntax, semantics. I analyzed a number of experimental studies, and inferred from their results the implications which seem relevant for the aesthetic theories. I will briefly review the conclusions reached in each chapter.

The first chapter dealt with the issue of meaning in music. The philosophers debated on whether meaning in music is achieved by the properties of musical structure alone, or by correspondences between the elements of musical structure and the extra-musical events and phenomena. It was also debated whether the kind of meaning which arises from music is primarily emotional, or specifically musical, formalistic meaning. I argued that, with the help of several experimental studies, it can be shown that solely by virtue of its structure, music is perceived by the listeners as possessing both formalistic and emotional meaning, but also conceptual meaning not mentioned in, or explicitly dismissed by the philosophical theories. I argued that musicological knowledge was necessary for a more sophisticated design of the experiments, and that this enabled conclusions regarding an important correlation between the expectations concerning musical structure and both the processing of meaning, and the emotional responses to the music. Finally, I combined the philosophical and the empirical conclusions to propose a way to understand the syntactic and the semantic level of musical structure alone.

In the second chapter, I argued that the dispositionalist view of musical value allowed forging connections between aesthetic value of musical works and the subjective reactions which can be tested experimentally. With the help of behavioral and neurological studies, I showed that even in very simple tasks concerning the detection, recognition, or differentiation of isolated musical elements, differences can be observed between the perceiving subjects, showing that trained musicians perform better compared to non-musicians. Neurological measures were immensely important in showing that the differences between these two groups of subjects occur already at the level of processing, and, more important, that the neurological differences between them are a result of neuroplasticity induced by musical training.

In the third chapter, I presented two most popular philosophical debates on the emotions in music, one concerning musical expressiveness, and the other concerning the possibility of musical induction of genuine emotions. The first debate was not very fruitful for the empirical research due to the (possibly inherent) vagueness of the term 'expressiveness'. Nevertheless, due to the similarity of expressiveness to musical meaning, I brought expressiveness into a relationship with the results of the study which showed that music can have extra-musical characteristics much broader than emotional characteristics (as postulated by the most of the philosophers), and that it can associate the listeners with – or express – not only emotional, but also conceptual content. I concluded that the empirical results offer a suggestion to the philosophers to consider the relationship between music and emotions not in isolation, but as a part of a broader network of associations between music and the extra-musical world. In regard to the second debate, the possibility to measure physiological components of the experienced emotions suggested that music does induce genuine emotions in the listeners. In addition, the strong physiological evidence of the emotional response to music helped to clarify that adopting a more general psychological theory of emotions determines the attitude toward the obtained empirical results. Thus the authors which take the combination of a subjective feeling and definite physiological indicators to be sufficient for an emotional experience, adopt these results as conclusive evidence for the emotivist side of the debate. Other authors, which believe that a definite cognitive aspect is highly significant for an experience to be considered a genuine emotion, consider the results as insufficient to support the emotivist view.

The Joint Implications of the Chapters

The most important point of this dissertation is, I believe, a methodological one. The methods used by the philosophers in order to construct their theories were mostly conceptual analysis (of concepts such as value, beauty, meaning), introspection (during listening to music, focusing on expectations, emotions, etc.), musicological analysis of musical works, phenomenological observation (of how we perceive musical works). On the other hand, the experimental research I presented relied on different methods and different kinds of facts. The experimental psychologists used, for example, several types of statistical methodology, such as partial correlation methodology, in which the the influence between the variables involved in the study is controlled or adjusted (e.g. changing the last chord of a musical sequence) in order to measure the relationship between the two target variables (such as expectedness of the chord and the reaction – neurological or emotional – of the subject). They also used case studies (such as studies of neurological and psychological disorders and how they differ in experience of music listening from the listeners without the given disorders). These experimental methods were used in combination with certain already known empirical facts which would by themselves seem meaningless to philosophers: for example, the *physiological* similarity between two brainwaves, or limitation of the neurological processing resources (Chapter 1, Section 2.1). Similarly to the philosophers, the experimental researchers also relied on their musicological knowledge, but used it differently – in designing experiments. This enabled a very sophisticated analysis of the correlations between musical events and the reactions of the subjects, for example, in constructing a *range* of musical unexpectedness according to the principles of harmonic distance, and then testing the correlations of unexpectedness with the degree of intensity of the emotions aroused by music

(Chapter 1, Section 2.2). Considering such methodological differences, it would be expected for the conclusions of the philosophers and of the experimental researchers to concern different, or even disparate aspects of music or the experience of listening to music. My dissertation has shown, however, that the results of the experimental research, unavailable to the armchair approach, can be taken as arguments relevant for the philosophical debates, even concerning the most abstract concepts such as meaning or value.

It is on the basis of the provided interdisciplinary conclusions that I disagree with Scruton's claim about the relevance of the experimental results for understanding our relationship with music: "Even if we came up with a theory about the processing of music, it would not, in itself, be an account of musical understanding. Indeed, it would tell us as little about the meaning and value of music as a cognitive model of mathematical understanding would tell us about the nature of mathematical truth. All the real problems, concerning what music means, why we enjoy it and why it is important to us, would remain untouched by such a theory."[412]

The results presented in the dissertation are by no means sufficient for resolving philosophical debates on musical meaning or value or the importance of music for humans. However, I believe that they are a good starting point for approaching the same old problems with new information at hand. Music is created by humans, for humans. Humans are the ones who give and find meaning and value in music. That is why I believe understanding how humans perceive and process music could be a rich source for understanding its meaning and value, although it should never be the only source. If the research is taken further in the same direction (as I am sure it will), it should bring us to an even better understanding of the relationship between human beings and the music that they create, appreciate and enjoy.

---

[412] Roger Scruton, *Music as an Art*, (London: Bloomsbury Continuum, 2018).

Limitations and Suggestions for Further Research

It should be acknowledged that there are still serious limitations in the scope of implications we can infer from the presented experimental results. Most of the studies used very simple stimuli, such as short musical sequences consisting solely of chords or melody lines. Some of the stimuli were as simple as single tones, or even frequencies presented in isolation. The tasks presented to the subjects were overly simple as well: they required recognizing whether the music sequences were same or different, or whether there was a slight irregularity in the sequence, etc. The studies mostly tested isolated cognitive capacities which are far from the complex capabilities necessary for understanding music and passing appropriate aesthetic judgments. Finally, the research on music preference in the aesthetically relevant sense are yet to be conducted. The worries addressed by the skeptics concerning the scientific approach to music (See Section 'Contemporary Attitudes' in the Introduction) that the scientific explanations might be musically or psychologically simplistic thus still hold to some extent. I believe, however, that the research presented in this dissertation provides a model for researching more complex tasks and capacities, which would be closer to the actual musical experiences. With more diverse, and larger scale stimuli, more similar to the actual musical works, and more complex and diverse tasks which resemble the process of actual aesthetic appreciation of musical works, we could arrive at more aesthetically relevant, non-reductionistic explanations of the musical experience. I believe that further empirical exploration of music should proceed in this direction, and along with further conceptual analyses it may lead to more interesting and more aesthetically relevant conclusions.

Further investigation could also examine the subjective reactions in the overlap of the philosophical topics presented in this dissertation. It would be interesting to examine the possible correlations between the emotions induced by music and the value attributed to the musical work, or whether the meaning perceived in music relates to the emotions felt as a response.

As already mentioned, aesthetics of music was chosen as a case study in order to examine the relationship between the normative philosophy and the experimental research. The methodological conclusions I reached are specifically focused on the aesthetic issues concerning music. It is not clear if similar methodological connections could be forged for other normative philosophical disciplines (such as ethics or politics), or even for other arts (especially literature). Nevertheless, the presented attempt at connecting disparate disciplines can serve as a general model for further analyses in this direction, and hopefully inspire philosophers to accept more unconventional approaches and search for the kinds of arguments unavailable from their respective disciplines.

Bibliography

- Allen, R. T. "The Arousal and Expression of Emotion by Music." *British Journal of Aesthetics* 30, no. 1 (1990): 57-61.

- Aristotle. *Politics*

- Aristoxenus. "Elementa Harmonica." In *Greek Musical Writings, Volume II: Harmonic and Acoustic Theory.* Edited by Andrew Barker, 126-190. Cambridge University Press, 1989.

- Atienza, Mercedes, Jose L. Cantero, and Elena Dominguez-Marin. "The Time Course of Neural Changes Underlying Auditory Perceptual Learning." *Learning and Memory* 9, no. 3 (2002): 138-150.

- Bartlett, Dale L. "Physiological Responses to Music and Sound Stimuli." In *Handbook of Music Psychology*, edited by Donald A. Hodges, 343-385. San Antonio, TX: Institute for Music Research Press, 1996.

- Beardsley, Monroe C. "Beauty and Aesthetic Value." *Journal of Philosophy* 59, no. 21 (1962):617-628.

- Benedeka, Mathias, and Christian Kaernbach. "A Continuous Measure of Phasic Electrodermal Activity." *Journal of Neuroscience Methods* 190, no.1 (2010): 80-91.

- Berlyne, Daniel E. *Studies in the New Experimental Aesthetics: Steps Towards an Objective Psychology of Aesthetic Appreciation.* London: Halstead press, 1974.

- Bharucha, Jamshed, and Carol L. Krumhansl. "The Representation of Harmonic Structure in Music: Hierarchies of Stability as a Function of Context." *Cognition* 13, no. 1 (1983), pp. 63-102.

- Bharucha, Jamshed, and Keiko Stoeckig. "Reaction Time and Musical Expectancy: Priming of Chords." *Journal of Experimental Psychology: Human Perception and Performance* 12, no. 4 (1986), pp. 403-410.

- Bigand, Emmanuel, Barbara Tillmann, Bénédicte Poulin-Charronnat, Daniel A. D'Adamo, and François Madurell. "The Effect of Harmonic Context on Phoneme Monitoring in Vocal Music." *Cognition* 81, no. 1 (2001): B11-B20.

- Bigand, Emmanuel, François Madurell, Barbara Tillmann, and Marion Pineau. "Effects of Global Structure and Temporal Organization on Chord Processing." *Journal of Experimental Psychology: Human Perception and Performance* 25 (1999):184-197.

- Bigand, Emmanuel, François Madurell, Barbara Tillmann, and Marion Pineau. "Effect of Global Structure and Temporal Organisation on Chord Processing." *Journal of Experimental Psychology: Human Perception and Performance* 2 (1999): 184-197.

- Bigand, Emmanuel, Richard Parncutt, and Fred Lerdahl. "Perception of Music Tension in Short Chord Sequences: the Influence of Harmonic Function, Sensory Dissonance, Horizontal Motion, and Musical Training." *Perception & Psychophysics* 58, no. 1 (1996):125-141.

- Boltz, Marilyn G. "The Generation of Temporal and Melodic Expectancies During Musical Listening." *Perception and Psychophysics* 53, no. 6 (1993): 585-600.

- Bradley, Margaret M., and Peter J. Lang. "Affective Reactions to Acoustic Stimuli." *Psychophysiology*, 37, (2000): 204-215.

- Bradley, Margaret M., and Peter J. Lang. "Affective Reactions to Acoustic Stimuli." *Psychophysiology* 37, no. 2 (2000): 204-215.

- Bradley, Margaret M., Peter J. Lang, and Bruce N. Cuthbert, "Emotion, Novelty, and the Startle Reflex: Habituation in Humans," *Behavioural Neuroscience*, 107, (1993): 970-980.

- Brattico, Elvira, and Marcus T. Pearce. "The Neuroaesthetics of Music." *Psychology of Aesthetics, Creativity, and the Arts* 7 (2013): 48-61.

- Brattico, Elvira, Mari Tervaniemi, Risto Näätänen, and Isabelle Peretz. "Musical Scale Properties are Automatically Processed in the Human Auditory Cortex." *Brain Research* 1117, no. 1 (2006): 162-174.

- Buck, Ross. "Social and Emotional Functions in Facial Expression and Communication: The Read-Out Hypothesis." *Biological Psychology* 38, no. 2-3 (1994): 95-115.

- Bullack, Antje, Niklas Büdenbender, Ingo Roden, and Gunter Kreutz. "Psychophysiological Responses to 'Happy' and 'Sad' Music: A Replication

Study." *Music Perception: An Interdisciplinary Journal* 35 no. 4 (2018): 502-517.

- Cacioppo, John T., David J. Klein, Gary G. Berntson, and Elaine Hatfield. "The Psychophysiology of Emotion." In *Handbook of Emotion*, edited by Michael Lewis and Jeannette M. Haviland, 119-142. New York: Guilford Press, 1993.

- Cacioppo, John T., Richard E. Petty, Mary E. Losch, and Hai Sook Kim. "Electromyographic Activity Over Facial Muscle Regions Can Differentiate the Valence and Intensity of Affective Reactions." *Journal of Personality and Social Psychology* 50, no. 2 (1986): 260-268.

- Callen, Donald. "The Sentiment in Musical Sensibility." *Journal of Aesthetics and Art Criticism* 40 (1982): 381-393.

- Carroll, Noël, Margaret Moore, and Willian P. Seeley. "The Philosophy of Art and Aesthetics, Psychology, and Neuroscience: Studies in Literature, Music, and Visual Arts." In *Aesthetic Science: Connecting Minds, Brains, and Experience*. Edited by Arthur P. Shimamura and Stephen E. Palmer, pp. 31-62. New York, NY: Oxford University Press, 2011.

- Chatterjee, Anjan. "Neuroaesthetics: A coming of age story." *Journal of Cognitive Neuroscience* 23 (2011): 53-62.

- Chen, Lei, Shuhua Zhou, and Jennings Bryant. "Temporal Changes in Mood Repair Through Music Consumption: Effects of Mood, Mood Salience, and Individual Differences." *Media Psychology* 9, (2007): 695-713.

- Cross, Ian, and Irène Deliège. "Introduction: Cognitive Science and Music – An Overview." *Contemporary Music Review*, 9:1-2, (1993): pp. 1-6.

- Cullari, Salvatore, and Olga Semanchick. "Music Preferences and Perception of Loudness." *Perceptual and Motor Skills* 68, no. 1 (1989): 186-186.

- David Huron. "Aesthetics." In *Oxford Handbook of Music Psychology*. Edited by Susan Hallam, Ian Cross, and Michael Thaut, pp. 151-162. New York, NY: Oxford University Press. 2010.

- Davies, Stephen. "Contra the Hypothetical Persona in Music", in Mette Hjort and Sue Laver (eds.), *Emotion and the Arts*, New York: Oxford UP, 1997.

- Davies, Stephen. "The Expression of Emotion in Music." *Mind* 89 (1980): 67-86.

- Davies, Stephen. *Musical Meaning and Expression*, Ithaca and London: Cornell UP, 1994.

- Dawe, Lloyd A., John R. Platt, and Ronald J. Racine. "Rhythm Perception and Differences in Accent Weights for Musicians and Nonmusicians." *Perception and Psychophysics* 57, no. 6 (1995): 905-914.

- Dennett, Daniel. *Consciousness Explained*. Boston: Little, Brown, 1991.

- Dimberg, Ulf. "Facial Reactions to Facial Expressions." *Psychophysiology* 19, no.6 (1982): 643-647.

- Eaton, Robert A. and Larry E. Roberts. "Effect of Spectral Frequency Discrimination on Auditory Transient and Steady State Responses in Humans." *Society for Neuroscience Abstracts* 29 (1999): 156.15.

- Ekman, Paul, Robert W. Levenson, and Wallace V. Friesen. "Autonomic Nervous System Activity Distinguishes Among Emotions." *Science* 221, no. 4616 (1983): 1208-1210.

- Ekman, Paul. "Facial Expression and Emotion." *American Psychologist* 48, no. 4 (1993): 384-392.

- Ekman, Paul. "Universal and Cultural Differences in Facial Expressions of Emotions." In *Nebraska Symposium on Motivation* 1971, edited by James K. Cole, 207-283. Lincoln, NE: University of Nebraska Press, 1972.

- Fridlund, Alan, Gary Schwartz, and Stephen Fowler. "Pattern Recognition of Self-Reported Emotional State From Multiple-Site Facial EMG Activity During Affective Imagery." *Psychophysiology* 21, no. 6 (1984): 622-637.

- Frijda, Nico H. "The Place of Appraisal in Emotion." *Cognition and Emotion* 7, no. 3-4 (1993):357-387.

- Gunter, Thomas, Angela Friederici, and Herbert Schriefers. "Syntactic Gender and Semantic Expectancy: ERPs Reveal Early Autonomy and Late Interaction." *Journal of Cognitive Neuroscience* 12, no. 4 (2000):556-568.

- Halpern, Andrea R., James C. Bartlett, and W. Jay Dowling. "Perception of Mode, Rhythm, and Contour in Unfamiliar Melodies: Effects of Age and Experience." *Music Perception: An Interdisciplinary Journal* 15, no. 4 (1998): 335-355.

- Hanslick, Eduard. *On the Musically Beautiful*. Translated by Geoffrey Payzant. Indianapolis: Hackett Publishing Company, 1986.

- Heyduk, Ronald G. "Rated Preference for Musical Compositions as it Relates to Complexity and Exposure Frequency." *Perception and Psychophysics* 17, no. 1 (1975): 84-90.

- Hietanen, Jari K., Viekko Surakka, and Ilkka Linnankoski. "Facial Electromyographic Responses to Vocal Affect Expressions." *Psychophysiology* 35, no. 5 (1998): 530-536.

- Hume, David. "Of the Standard of taste." In *Essays Moral, Political, and Literary*, edited by T. H. Green and T. H. Grose, 266-284. London, 1882.

- Hume, David. *Treatise of Human Nature.* Reprinted from the Original Edition in three volumes and edited by L.A. Selby-Bigge, M.A., Oxford: Clarendon Press, 1896.

- Izard, Carroll E. *Human emotions.* New York: Plenum, 1977.

- Jäncke, Lutz, Joachim Vogt, Frauke Musial, Kai Lutz, and Karl Theodor Kalveram. "Facial EMG Responses to Auditory Stimuli." *International Journal of Psychophysiology* 22, no 1-2 (1996): 85-96.

- Jones, Mari, Marilyn Boltz, and Gary R. Kidd. "Controlled Attending as a Function of Melodic and Temporal Context." *Perception and Psychophysics* 32, no. 3 (1982): 211-218.

- Juslin, Patrik and Petri Laukka. "Communication of Emotions in Vocal Expression and Music Performance: Different Channels, Same Code?." *Psychological Bulletin* 129, no. 5 (2003): 770-814.

- Juslin, Patrik, and John Sloboda. *Music and Emotion: Theory and Research.* New York: Oxford University Press, 2001.

- Juslin, Patrik, and Petri Laukka. "Expression, Perception, and Induction of Musical Emotions: A Review and a Questionnaire Study of Everyday Listening." *Journal of New Music Research* 33, no. 3 (2004): 217-238.

- Juslin, Patrik. "Cue Utilization in Communication of Emotion in Music Performance: Relating Performance to Perception." *Journal of Experimental Psychology: Human Perception and Performance* 26 (2000): 1797-1813.

- Kannyo, Irene, and Caroline M. DeLong. "The Effect of Musical Training on Auditory Perception." *The Journal of the Acoustical Society of America* 130, no. 4 (2011): 24-28.

- Kant, Immanuel. *Critique of Practical Reason*. Edited by Mary J. Gregor. Cambridge: Cambridge University Press, 1788/1997.
- Kant, Immanuel. *Critique of the Power of Judgment*. Translated by Paul Guyer and Eric Matthews. Cambridge: Cambridge University Press, 2000.
- Karl, Gregory and Jenefer Robinson. "Shostakovich's Tenth Symphony and the Musical Expression of Cognitively Complex Emotions." *Journal of Aesthetics and Art Criticism*, 53 (1995): 401-415.
- Kellaris, James J. "Consumer Aesthetics Outside the Lab: Preliminary Report on a Musical Field Study." *Advances in Consumer Research* 19 (1992): 730-734.
- Kivy, Peter. *Introduction to a Philosophy of Music*. Oxford: Clarendon Press, 2002.
- Kivy, Peter. *Sound Sentiment: An Essay on the Musical Emotions, Including the Complete Text of The Corded Shell*. Philadelphia: Temple University Press, 1989.
- Koch, Heinrich Christoph. "Introductory Essay on Composition (1787)." in *Aesthetics and the Art of Musical Composition in the German Enlightenment: Selected Writings of Johann Georg Sulzer and Heinrich Christoph Koch*, ed. Nancy Baker, Thomas Christensen, pp. 144-188. Cambridge University Press, 2006.
- Koelsch, Stefan, and Juul Mulder, "Electric Brain Responses to Inappropriate Harmonies During Listening to Expressive Music," *Clinical Neurophysiology* 113, no. 6 (2002): 862-869.
- Koelsch, Stefan, and Walter Siebel. "Towards a Neural Basis of Music Perception." *Trends in Cognitive Science* 9, no. 12 (2005): 578-584.
- Koelsch, Stefan, Elisabeth Kasper, Daniela Sammler, Katrin Schulze, Thomas Gunter, and Angela D Friederici. "Music, Language and Meaning: Brain Signatures of Semantic Processing," *Nature Neuroscience* 7 (2004): 302-7.
- Koelsch, Stefan, Erich Schröger, and Mari Tervaniemi, "Superior Pre-Attentive Auditory Processing in Musicians," *NeuroReport: For Rapid Communication of Neuroscience Research*, 10, no. 6 (1999): 1309-1313.

- Koelsch, Stefan, Thomas Gunter, Angela Friederici, and Erich Schroeger. "Brain Indices of Musical Processing: 'Nonmusicians' are Musical." *Journal of Cognitive Neuroscience* 12, no. 3 (2000): 520-541.

- Koelsch, Stefan, Thomas Gunter, Erich Schroeger, and Angela Friederici. "Processing Tonal Modulations: An ERP Study." *Journal of Cognitive Neuroscience* 15, no. 8 (2003): 1149-1159.

- Koelsch, Stefan, Thomas Gunter, Matthias Wittfoth, and Daniela Sammler. "Interaction in Syntax Processing in Language and Music: an ERP Study." *Journal of Cognitive Neuroscience* 17, no. 10 (2005): 1565-1577.

- Koelsch, Stefan. "Brain Correlates of Music-Evoked Emotions." *Nature Reviews Neuroscience* 15, no. 3 (2014): 170-180.

- Koelsch, Stefan. "Music-Evoked Emotions: Principles, Brain Correlates, and Implications for Therapy." *Annals of the New York Academy of Sciences* 1337 (2015): 193-201.

- Kojen, Leon. "Hume On the Standard of Taste" ["Hjum o merilu ukusa"]. In *Art and Value* [*Umetnost i vrednost*], 153-207. Beograd: Filip Višnjić, 1989.

- Konečni, Vladimir. "Does Music Induce Emotion? A Theoretical and Methodological Analysis." *Psychology of Aesthetics Creativity and the Arts* 2, no. 2 (2008): 115-129.

- Krumhansl, Carol L. "A Perceptual Analysis of Mozart's Piano Sonata K. 282: Segmentation, Tension and Musical Ideas." *Music Perception* 13, no. 3 (1996): 401-432.

- Krumhansl, Carol L. "An Exploratory Study of Musical Emotions and Psychophysiology." *Canadian Journal of Experimental Psychology* 51, no. 4 (1997): 336-352.

- Krumhansl, Carol L. "Music: A Link Between Cognition and Emotion." *Current Directions in Psychological Science*, 11, no. 2 (2002): 45-50.

- Krumhansl, Carol L. "Topic in Music: An Empirical Study of Memorability, Openness, and Emotion in Mozart's String Quartet in C major and Beethoven's String Quartet in A minor." *Music Perception* 16 (1998): 119-134.

- Krumhansl, Carol L., and Diana Lynn Schenck. "Can Dance Reflect the Structural and Expressive Qualities of Music? A Perceptual Experiment on

Balanchine's Choreography of Mozart's Divertimento No. 15." *Musicae Scientiae* 1 (1997): 63-85.

- Krumhansl, Carol L.. "The Psychological Representation of Musical Pitch in a Tonal Context." *Cognitive Psychology*, 11 (1979): 346-347.

- Kutas, Marta, and Kara D Federmeier. "Electrophysiology Reveals Semantic Memory Use in Language Comprehension." *Trends in Cognitive Sciences* 4, no. 12 (2000):463-470.

- Lamont, Alexandra, and Rebecca Webb. "Short- and Long-Term Musical Preferences: What Makes a Favourite Piece of Music?" *Psychology of Music* 38, no. 2 (2010): 222–241.

- Lerdahl, Fred, and Ray Jackendoff. *A Generative Theory of Tonal Music*. Cambridge (MA): MIT Press, 1983.

- Levenson, Robert W. "Human Emotion: A Functional View." In *The Nature of Emotion: Fundamental Questions*, edited by Paul Ekman and Richard J. Davidson, 123-126. New York: Oxford University Press, 1994.

- Levenson, Robert W., Paul Ekman, and Wallace V. Friesen. "Voluntary Facial Action Generates Emotion-Specific Autonomic Nervous System Activity." *Psychophysiology* 27, no. 4 (1990): 363-384.

- Leventhal, Howard. "A Perceptual-Motor Theory of Emotion." *Information (International Social Science Council)* 21, no. 6 (1982): 819-845.

- Levinson, Jerrold. "Hope in The Hebrides." In *Music, Art, and Metaphysics*, 336-75. Ithaca, NY: Cornell University Press, 1990.

- Levitin, Daniel J., and Anna K. Tirovolas, "Current Advances in the Cognitive Neuroscience of Music" *Annals of the New York Academy of Sciences* 1156 (2009): 211–231.

- Lonsdale, Adam J., and Adrian C. North. "Why Do We Listen to Music? A Uses and Gratifications Analysis." *British Journal of Psychology* 102 (2011): 108-134.

- Loui, Psyche, Tineke Grent-'t-Jong, Dana Torpey, and MartyWoldorff. "Effects of Attention on the Neural Processing of Harmonic Syntax in Western Music." *Cognitive Brain Research* 25, no. 3 (2005):678-687.

- Lundqvist, Lars-Olov, and Ulf Dimberg. "Facial Expressions Are Contagious." *Journal of Psychophysiology* 9, no. 2 (1995): 203-211.

- Lundqvist, Lars-Olov, Fredrik Carlsson, Per Hilmersson, and Patrik N. Juslin. "Emotional Responses to Music: Experience, Expression, and Physiology." *Psychology of Music* 37, no. 1 (2009): 61-90.

- Lundqvist, Lars-Olov. "Facial EMG Reactions to Facial Expressions: A Case of Facial Emotional Contagion?" *Scandinavian Journal of Psychology* 36(2), (1995): 130-141.

- Madsen, Clifford K. "Modulated Beat Discrimination among Musicians and Nonmusicians." *Journal of Research in Music Education* 27, no. 2 (1979): 57-67.

- Martindale, Colin, and Kathleen Moore. "Relationship of Musical Preference to Collative, Ecological, and Psychophysical Variables," *Music Perception* 6, no. 4 (1989): 431-445.

- Mattheson, Johann. *Johann Mattheson's Der vollkommene Capellmeister: a Revised Translation with Critical Commentary*. Edited and translated by Ernest C. Harriss and Ann Arbor. Mich: UMI Research Press, c1981.

- Mauss, Iris B., Robert W. Levenson, Loren McCarter, Frank H. Wilhelm, James J. Gross. "The Tie That Binds? Coherence Among Emotion Experience, Behavior, and Physiology." *Emotion* 5, no. 2 (2005): 175-190.

- Mew, Peter. "The Expression of Emotion in Music." *British Journal of Aesthetics* 25 (1985): 33-42.

- Mew, Peter. "The Musical Arousal of Emotions." *British Journal of Aesthetics* 25 (1985): 357-361.

- Meyer, Leonard B. *Emotion and Meaning in Music*. Chicago: University of Chicago Press, 1956.

- Morrow, Daniel, Von Leirer, Patsy Altieri, and Colleen Fitzsimmons. "When Expertise Reduces Age Differences in Performance." *Psychology and Aging* 9, no. 1 (1994): 134-148.

- Müller, Mira, Lea Höfel, Elvira Brattico, and Thomas Jacobsen. "Aesthetic Judgments of Music in Experts and Laypersons – An ERP Study." *International Journal of Psychophysiology* 76, no. 1 (2010): 40-51.

- Näätänen, Risto, Petri Paavilainen, Hannu Tiitinen, Deming Jiang, and Kimmo Alho. "Attention and Mismatch Negativity." *Psychophysiology* 30, no. 5 (1993): 436-450.

- Narmour, Eugene. *The Analysis and Cognition of Basic Melodic Structures.* Chicago: University of Chicago Press, 1990.
- Noë, Alva. "Art and the Limits of Neuroscience." *New York Times*, Dec. 4, 2011.
- Nolt, John. "Expression and Emotions." *British Journal of Aesthetics* 21 (1981): 139-150.
- North, Adrian C., and David J. Hargreaves. "Situational Influences on Reported Musical Preference." *Psychomusicology* 15, no. 1-2 (1996): 30-45.
- Nyklíček, Ivan, Julian F. Thayer, Lorenz J. P. Van Doornen. "Cardiorespiratory differentiation of musically induced emotions." *Journal of Psychophysiology* 11, no. 4 (1997): 304-321.
- Pantev, Christo, Robert Oostenveld, Almut Engelien, Bernhard Ross, Larry E. Roberts, and Manfried Hoke. "Increased Auditory Cortical Representation in Musicians." *Nature* 392 (1998): 811-814.
- Patel, Aniruddh D, Edward Gibson, Jennifer Ratner, Mireille Besson, Phillip Holcomb. "Processing Syntactic Relations in Language and Music: An Event-Related Potential Study." *Journal of Cognitive Neuroscience* 10, no. 6 (1998): 717-733.
- Patel, Aniruddh D. "Language, Music, Syntax and the Brain." *Nature Neuroscience* 6, no. 7 (2003): 674-681.
- Pearce, Marcus T., Dahlia W. Zaidel, Oshin Vartanian, Martin Skov, Helmut Leder, Anjan Chatterjee, and Marcos Nadal. "Neuroaesthetics: The Cognitive Neuroscience of Aesthetic Experience." *Perspectives on Psychological Science* 11, no. 2 (2016): 265-279.
- Pinker, Steven. *How The Mind Works.* London: Allen Lane, 1997.
- Pitt, Mark A. "Perception of Pitch and Timbre by Musically Trained and Untrained Listeners." *Journal of Experimental Psychology: Human Perception and Performance* 20, no. 5 (1994): 976-986.
- Plato. *Republic*
- Poulin-Charronat, Bénédicte, Emmanuel Bigand, and Stefan Koelsch. "Processing of Musical Syntax Tonic versus Subdominant: An Event-Related Potential Study." *Journal of Cognitive Neuroscience* 18, no. 9 (2006):1545-1554.

- Reisberg, Daniel. *Cognition: Exploring the Science of the Mind*. New York: W. W. Norton & Company, Inc., 2007.

- Richards, Ivor Armstrong. *Poetries and Sciences: A Reissue with a Commentary of Science and Poetry* (1926, 1935). New York: W. W. Norton and Company, 1970.

- Robinson, Jenefer. *Deeper than Reason: Emotion and its Role in Literature, Music and Art*. Oxford: Clarendon Press, 2005.

- Salganik, Matthew J., Peter S. Dodds, and Duncan J. Watts. "Experimental Study of Inequality and Unpredictability in an Artificial Cultural Market." *Science* 311 (2006): 854-856.

- Schaefer, Thomas. "Determinants of Music Preference." PhD diss., Chemnitz University, 2008.

- Scherer, Klaus R. "Why Music does not Produce Basic Emotions: Pleading for a New Approach to Measuring the Emotional Effects of Music." In *Proceedings of the Stockholm Music Acoustics Conference*, ed. Roberto Bresin (Stockholm, Sweden: Royal Institute of Technology, 2003), 25-28.

- Schmuckler, Mark A. "Expectation in Music: Investigation of Melodic and Harmonic Processes." *Music Perception*, 7, no. 2 (1989): 109-150.

- Schwartz, Gary E., Paul L. Fair, Patricia Salt, Michel R. Mandel, Gerald L. Klerman. "Facial Muscle Patterning to Affective Imagery in Depressed and Nondepressed Subjects." *Science* 192, no. 4238 (1976): 489-491.

- Scruton, Roger. *Music as an Art*. London: Bloomsbury Continuum, 2018.

- Seither Preisler, Annemarie, Linda Johnson, Katrin Krumbholz, Andrea Nobbe, Roy Patterson, Stefan Seither, and Bernd Lütkenhöner. "Tone Sequences With Conflicting Fundamental Pitch and Timbre Changes Are Heard Differently by Musicians and Nonmusicians." *Journal of Experimental Psychology: Human Perception and Performance* 33, no. 3 (2007): 743-51.

- Shahin, Antoine, Daniel J. Bosnyak, Laurel J. Trainor and Larry E. Roberts. "Enhancement of Neuroplastic P2 and N1c Auditory Evoked Potentials in Musicians." *Journal of Neuroscience* 23, no. 13 (2003): 5545-5552.

- Sittiprapaporn, Wichian, and Jun Soo Kwon. "Brain Electric Microstate and Perception of Simultaneously Audiovisual Presentation." in Artificial Neural

Networks – ICANN 2009, 19th International Conference, Limassol, Cyprus, September 14-17, 2009, Proceedings, Part I.

- Sleigh, Merry J., and Jordan McElroy. "The Effect of Music Listening Versus Written Reframing on Mood Management." *Music Perception* 31 (2014): 303-315.

- Slevc, Robert L., Jason C. Rosenberg, and Aniruddh D. Patel. "Making Psycholinguistics Musical: Self-Paced Reading Time Evidence for Shared Processing of Linguistic and Musical Syntax." *Psychonomic Bulletin & Review* 16, no. 2 (2009): 374-381.

- Sloboda, John A. "Cognition and Real Music: The Psychology of Music Comes of Age." *Psychologica Belgica* 26 (1986): 199-219.

- Smith, Craig A. and Richard S. Lazarus. "Appraisal Components, Core Relational Themes, and the Emotions." *Cognition and Emotion* 7, no. 3-4 (1993): 233-269.

- Smith, David J., and Robert J. Melara. "Aesthetic Preference and Syntactic Prototypicality in Music: Tis the Gift to be Simple." *Cognition* 34, no. 3 (1990): 279-298.

- Speck, Stanley. "Arousal Theory' Reconsidered." *British Journal of Aesthetics* 28 (1988): 40-47.

- Srećković, Sanja. „Eduard Hanslick's Formalism and His Most Influential Contemporary Critics." *Belgrade Philosophical Annual* 27 (2014): 113-134.

- Steinbeis, Nikolaus, and Stefan Koelsch. "Shared Neural Resources between Music and Language Indicate Semantic Processing of Musical Tension-Resolution Patterns," *Cerebral Cortex* 18, no. 5 (2008): 1169-78.

- Steinbeis, Nikolaus, Stefan Koelsch, and John Sloboda. "The Role of Harmonic Expectancy Violations in Musical Emotions: Evidence from Subjective, Physiological, and Neural Responses," *Journal of Cognitive Neuroscience* 18, no. 8 (2006): 1380-93.

- Sulzer, Johann Georg. "General Theory of the Fine Arts (1771-74): Selected Articles." In *Aesthetics and the Art of Musical Composition in the German Enlightenment: Selected Writings of Johann Georg Sulzer and Heinrich Christoph Koch*, edited by Nancy Baker, Thomas Christensen, pp. 25-111. Cambridge University Press, 2006.

- Swathi Swaminathan and E. Glenn Schellenberg, "Current Emotion Research in Music Psychology," *Emotion Review* 7, no. 2 (2015): 189-197.

- Tallis, Raymond. "The Limitations of a Neurological Approach to Art." *The Lancet* 372 (2008): 19-20.

- Tatarkiewicz, Wladyslaw. "Objectivity and Subjectivity in the History of Aesthetics." *Philosophy and Phenomenological Research* 24, no. 2 (1963): 157-173.

- Tatarkiewicz, Wladyslaw. *A History of Six Ideas: An Essay in Aesthetics.* Polish Scientific Publishers-Warszawa, 1980.

- Thayer, Julian F. "Multiple Indicators Of Affective Response To Music." PhD diss., New York University, 1986.

- Tillmann, Barbara, Jamshed Bharucha, and Emmanuel Bigand. "Implicit Learning of Tonality: A Self-Organizing Approach." *Psychological Review* 107, no. 4 (2000): 885-913.

- Toiviainen, Petri, and Carol L. Krumhansl. "Measuring and Modelling Real-Time Responses to Music: The Dynamics of Tonality Induction." *Perception* 32, no. 6 (2003): 741-766.

- Tremblay, Kelly, Nina Kraus, Therese McGee, Curtis Ponton, and Brian Otis. "Central Auditory Plasticity: Changes in the N1-P2 Complex After Speech-Sound Training." *Ear and Hearing* 22, no. 2 (2001):79-90.

- Tullman, Katherine,and Nada Gatalo. "Cave Paintings, Neuroaesthetics and Everything in Between: An Interview With Noël Carroll." *Postgraduate Journal of Aesthetics* 9, no. 1, 2012.

- Ullman, Michael. "A Neurocognitive Perspective on Language: The Declarative/Procedural Model." *Nature reviews Neuroscience* 2 (2001): 717-726.

- Van Der Zwaag, Marjolein, Joyce Westerink, and Egon L. van den Broek. "Emotional and Psychophysiological Responses to Tempo, Mode, and Percussiveness." *Musicae Scientiae* 15, no. 2 (2011): 250-269.

- Van Petten, Cyma, and Marta Kutas. "Interactions Between Sentence Context and Word Frequency in Event-Related Brain Potentials." *Memory and Cognition* 18, no. 4 (1990):380-393.

- von Ehrenfels, Christian. "On Gestalt qualities." In *Foundations of Gestalt Theory*. Edited by Barry Smith, Munich: Philosphia Verlag, 1988 (Original work published in 1890).
- Waterman, Mitch. "Emotional Responses to Music: Implicit and Explicit Effects in Listeners and Performers." *Psychology of Music* 24, no. 1 (1996): 53-67.
- Witvliet, Charlotte van Oyen, and Scott R. Vrana. "The Emotional Impact of Instrumental Music on Affect Ratings, Facial EMG, Autonomic Measures, and the Startle Reflex: Effects of Valence and Arousal." *Psychophysiology Supplement* 91 (1996).
- Wozniak, Robert H. "Introduction to Elemente der Psychophysik." In *Classics in Psychology, 1855-1914: Historical Essays.* Edited by Robert H. Wozniak, Bristol, UK: Thoemmes Press, 1999.

Biografija autora

Sanja Srećković rođena je 1987. godine u Beogradu. Osnovne studije upisala je na Filozofskom fakultetu u Beogradu na smeru filozofija 2006, a završila je 2011. godine. Naslov njenog završnog rada je "Specifično iskustvo vremena u muzici perioda fin-de-siècle: relativizacija uloge forme na primeru značaja teme u Regerovim Varijacijama za klavir h-moll na temu J. S. Bacha, op. 81", a mentor je bio prof. dr Miloš Arsenijević. Tokom osnovnih studija ostvarila je prosečnu ocenu 9,73. Studije drugog stepena završila je 2014. na Odeljenju za filozofiju Filozofskog fakulteta u Beogradu sa master tezom "Hanslikov formalizam i njegovi najuticajniji savremeni kritičari" kod prof. dr Miloša Arsenijevića. Za vreme osnovnih i master studija primala je stipendiju Fonda za mlade talente Ministarstva omladine i sporta Republike Srbije. Prosečna ocena na master studijama je 10. Doktorske studije na istom fakultetu upisala je 2014. godine. U periodu od 2011. do 2017. bila je angažovana kao saradnik u nastavi na Odeljenju za filozofiju na sledećim predmetima: Istorija filozofije 2a, Kantova filozofija, Metodika nastave filozofije sa osnovama filozofije obrazovanja 1 i 2, Ranohrišćanska i srednjovekovna filozofija. Od 2017. angažovana je na projeku „Logičko-epistemološki osnovi nauke i metafizike", čiji rukovodilac je prof. dr Miloš Arsenijević. Takođe 2017. izabrana je u zvanje istraživača saradnika na Institutu za filozofiju Filozofskog fakulteta u Beogradu, gde je od iste godine i zaposlena.

Sanja Srećković je učestvovala na više međunarodnih simpozijuma i konferencija: „Isečak filozofiranja o muzici: od umetničke igre tonova do muzičke igre emocija" na Tribini Instituta za filozofiiju i društvenu teoriju Univerziteta u Beogradu (2015); „Eduard Hanslick's formalism and his most influential contemporary critics" na 17th Edition of the International Conference: Contemporary Philosophical Issues, u Rijeci (2015); „Teorijsko-praktična polemika u estetici muzike" na 16. Međunarodnoj filozofskoj školi Felix Romuliana, u Zaječaru (2015); „Lažni temelji savremene estetike muzike: prividno odbacivanje tradicije" na 22. Filozofskom simpozijumu, u Sremskim Karlovcima (2015); „Empirical musicology vs. Mathematical Harmony: Two Images of Music that Modified the Music", na Transpositions: Music/Image,

XIII. International Conference of the Department of Musicology, Fakulteta muzičke umetnosti u Beogradu (2016); "Experiments in Cognitive Science: Reasoning in Non-linguistic Creatures", na 3rd Belgrade Conference in Analytic Philosophy, Univerzitet u Beogradu (2018); "Eksperimenti sa životinjama i malom decom: Mišljenje u odsustvu jezika", na tribini Moralna i zakonska prava životinja, u Beogradu (2018); "Analyzing the Results of Experimental Psychology: Reasoning in Non- and Pre-linguistic Creatures", na 26th Conference of the European Society for Philosophy and Psychology (ESPP), Rijeka, (2018); "Musical Sensitivity, Preferences and Emotional Responses", na Words, Music and Gender conference, Univerziteta u Mariboru (2019); "Filozofija, muzika i naučni eksperimenti: Šta znači muzika?" na Interdisciplinarnom seminaru društvenih i humanističkih nauka (DRH), u Petnici (2019); "Contribution of Neuropsychological Research to the Philosophical Debates on Musical Meaning", kao predstavnik Srbije na Third EECP Workshop, u Bratislavi (2019); "The Role of Emotions in the Appraisal of Music" na Philosophy of Emotions, York University's 11th Annual Philosophy Graduate Conference, York University, u Torontu (2019); "Music in the Context of Cognitive Science", na Contextuality of Musicology – What, How, Why and Because, XIV. International Conference of the Department of Musicology, Fakulteta muzičke umetnosti u Beogradu (2018); "Music in the Imagination of Ancient Philosophers", na Conference on Philosophical Imagination, Thought Experiments and Arguments in Antiquity, na Univerzitetu u Mariboru, (2018); "Bridging the Gap Between Experimental Psychology and Normative Philosophy: a Case Study in Musical Aesthetics", na The 27th Annual Meeting of the European Society for Philosophy and Psychology (ESPP), u Atini (2019); "Psychological Research and Philosophical Debates on Musical Meaning", prihvaćena je za izlaganje na Psychology and Music: Interdisciplinary Encounters, u Beogradu (oktobar 2019);

Sanja je do sada publikovala nekoliko radova: u časopisu Belgrade Philosophical Annual objavila je svoju master tezu "Eduard Hanslick's formalism and his most influential contemporary critics" (2014) i "Reasoning of Non- and Pre-Linguistic Creatures: How Much Do the Experiments Tell Us?" (2018); U časopisu Theoria objavila je "Muzička ekspresivnost" (2015).

Изјава о ауторству

Име и презиме аутора ___Сања Срећковић_____

Број индекса _____ОФ14-10_____

Изјављујем

да је докторска дисертација под насловом

Музика између филозофије и науке: применљивост резултата научних
истраживања у филозофији музике
(Music between philosophy and science: The applicability of scientific results to the
philosophy of music)

- резултат сопственог истраживачког рада;
- да дисертација у целини ни у деловима није била предложена за стицање друге дипломе према студијским програмима других високошколских установа;
- да су резултати коректно наведени и
- да нисам кршио/ла ауторска права и користио/ла интелектуалну својину других лица.

Потпис аутора

У Београду, _____

_____

Изјава о истоветности штампане и електронске верзије докторског рада

Име и презиме аутора _____ Сања Срећковић _____

Број индекса _____ 0Ф 14-10 _____

Студијски програм _____ Философија _____

Наслов рада __ **Музика између философије и науке: применљивост** _____
резултата научних истраживања у философији музике _____
(Music between philosophy and science: The applicability of scientific results to the
philosophy of music) _____

Ментор _____ др Милош Арсенијевић _____

Изјављујем да је штампана верзија мог докторског рада истоветна електронској верзији коју сам предао/ла ради похрањена у **Дигиталном репозиторијуму Универзитета у Београду**.

Дозвољавам да се објаве моји лични подаци везани за добијање академског назива доктора наука, као што су име и презиме, година и место рођења и датум одбране рада.

Ови лични подаци могу се објавити на мрежним страницама дигиталне библиотеке, у електронском каталогу и у публикацијама Универзитета у Београду.

Потпис аутора

У Београду, _____

_____

Изјава о коришћењу

Овлашћујем Универзитетску библиотеку „Светозар Марковић" да у Дигитални репозиторијум Универзитета у Београду унесе моју докторску дисертацију под насловом:

Музика између филозофије и науке: применљивост резултата научних истраживања у филозофији музике
(Music between philosophy and science: The applicability of scientific results to the philosophy of music)

која је моје ауторско дело.

Дисертацију са свим прилозима предао/ла сам у електронском формату погодном за трајно архивирање.

Моју докторску дисертацију похрањену у Дигиталном репозиторијуму Универзитета у Београду и доступну у отвореном приступу могу да користе сви који поштују одредбе садржане у одабраном типу лиценце Креативне заједнице (Creative Commons) за коју сам се одлучио/ла.

1. Ауторство (CC BY)

2. Ауторство – некомерцијално (CC BY-NC)

3. Ауторство – некомерцијално – без прерада (CC BY-NC-ND)

4. Ауторство – некомерцијално – делити под истим условима (CC BY-NC-SA)

5. Ауторство – без прерада (CC BY-ND)

6. Ауторство – делити под истим условима (CC BY-SA)

(Молимо да заокружите само једну од шест понуђених лиценци.
Кратак опис лиценци је саставни део ове изјаве).

Потпис аутора

У Београду, _____

1. **Ауторство**. Дозвољавате умножавање, дистрибуцију и јавно саопштавање дела, и прераде, ако се наведе име аутора на начин одређен од стране аутора или даваоца лиценце, чак и у комерцијалне сврхе. Ово је најслободнија од свих лиценци.

2. **Ауторство – некомерцијално**. Дозвољавате умножавање, дистрибуцију и јавно саопштавање дела, и прераде, ако се наведе име аутора на начин одређен од стране аутора или даваоца лиценце. Ова лиценца не дозвољава комерцијалну употребу дела.

3. **Ауторство – некомерцијално – без прерада**. Дозвољавате умножавање, дистрибуцију и јавно саопштавање дела, без промена, преобликовања или употребе дела у свом делу, ако се наведе име аутора на начин одређен од стране аутора или даваоца лиценце. Ова лиценца не дозвољава комерцијалну употребу дела. У односу на све остале лиценце, овом лиценцом се ограничава највећи обим права коришћења дела.

4. **Ауторство – некомерцијално – делити под истим условима**. Дозвољавате умножавање, дистрибуцију и јавно саопштавање дела, и прераде, ако се наведе име аутора на начин одређен од стране аутора или даваоца лиценце и ако се прерада дистрибуира под истом или сличном лиценцом. Ова лиценца не дозвољава комерцијалну употребу дела и прерада.

5. **Ауторство – без прерада**. Дозвољавате умножавање, дистрибуцију и јавно саопштавање дела, без промена, преобликовања или употребе дела у свом делу, ако се наведе име аутора на начин одређен од стране аутора или даваоца лиценце. Ова лиценца дозвољава комерцијалну употребу дела.

6. **Ауторство – делити под истим условима**. Дозвољавате умножавање, дистрибуцију и јавно саопштавање дела, и прераде, ако се наведе име аутора на начин одређен од стране аутора или даваоца лиценце и ако се прерада дистрибуира под истом или сличном лиценцом. Ова лиценца дозвољава комерцијалну употребу дела и прерада. Слична је софтверским лиценцама, односно лиценцама отвореног кода.

Ingram Content Group UK Ltd.
Milton Keynes UK
UKHW020628120623
423291UK00013B/550